# *Lord, You Must Be Joking!*

## Bible Stories That Tell *Your* Story

**Eugene J. Webb**

Resource Publications, Inc.
San Jose, California

Editorial director: Kenneth Guentert
Managing editor: Elizabeth J. Asborno
Editorial assistant: Rock Palladino

Reprint Department
Resource Publications, Inc.
160 E. Virginia Street #290
San Jose, CA 95112-5876

**Library of Congress Cataloging in Publication Data**
Webb, Eugene J., 1940-
    Lord, you must be joking! : Bible stories that tell your story / Eugene J. Webb.
        p.    cm.
    ISBN 0-89390-309-4
    Includes indexes.
    1. Bible stories, English. I. Title.
BS550.2.W36 1994
242'.5—dc20                                                    94-22722

Printed in the United States of America

98 97 96 95 94 | 5 4 3 2 1

To the people who live in the stories of the bible:
I thank them for clamoring at my door,
asking for a chance to be heard.


To the people who daily seek my counsel,
who bless me with the richness of their stories,
and who allow me to bless them with the humor
already contained in their lives.


To our four children,
Kristen, Douglas, Kevin and Jennifer—
the best stories my wife and I ever created.


To Marty, whose help and counsel
on this work I value and respect.

# Contents

# Preface

# *Bible Stories That Tell* Your *Story*

"Jesus and I have the same problem," mused my eight-year-old son as we were driving home from church one beautiful Sunday morning.

"How's that?" I asked, not knowing to what he was referring, but bracing myself for another of his insightful glimpses of life.

"*You* know, Dad. The story at church today. How Jesus fed all those people."

"I don't get it," I pursued. "What problem did he have?"

"Well," my son continued, "Jesus had trouble with numbers, like I do. 'Cause if he would have counted how many people were staying for dinner, he would never have been able to make the fish and bread stretch that far!"

I darn near lost control of the truck. I laughed till my stomach hurt. He joined in the laughter as well, for he too suddenly saw the humor of his conclusion.

For the rest of the day, I reflected on Jesus' invitation that we be as children in order to recognize the kingdom he so often talked about; I pondered how he did not exclude his own message from that child-like vision. He lived and told his own story. He predicted that his story would be retold and relived with each telling. And he warned his listeners that if they took any story, especially *the* story of God's covenant with humanity, too seriously, they would become hostages held to the literal rendering of the story. He scolded them that they, by being so serious, so literal, had missed the spirit, the aliveness, the passion of sacred scripture. They never got it!

/ Throughout my life of reading and re-reading sacred scripture, I have never ceased to be amazed at Jesus' use of stories not only to make a point but also to provoke, to challenge, to confound, and yes, to entertain his listeners. He loved the use of puns, played with metaphors, teased with paradoxes, exaggerated drama, and stole the show with humor. And nothing in his style was in opposition with the deliberateness of his intent: to stretch the imagination of his listeners and to prepare the human ground for spiritual awakening.

Now, what do *you* do when you tell your story to someone? You have a choice:

A. You can relate your personal experience in a serious monotone of so-called "facts," groping for accuracy, searching for proofs and thus duplicating your last telling and "freezing" the experience in time. Seriousness plus literalness equal sameness equal deadness. Your audience yawns; you consider repeating yourself.

B. You (re)tell your story with a slightly altered sequence of events, an added touch of drama here and there, a bit of color, a dash of flavor—though the message remains substantially intact. And shazam! Your story comes alive, your audience is engaged, an air of excitement is about, and the doorway of relevance and human inspiration swings open. And should you and your listener catch the fire of that moment, you both see standing in the doorway a surprise visitor: Humor.

The choice is yours.

Humor is not a joke. It is not slapstick nor a put-down nor a demeaning glance. Humor is not an add-on, a postfactum bit of sarcasm or ridicule. Rather, humor is, as its root meaning suggests, the juiciness of a story, the aliveness of an experience. Humor is contained inside our humanity and must be teased out in order to be relished.

This teasing out of humor can occur instantly when we step from inside of an experience and look back on it from *outside*. If I am driving a freeway and not being allowed to change lanes by discourteous drivers, that is a routine, serious event. However, in the telling of this experience, the event becomes: "You wouldn't believe this eighteen wheeler that almost ran me over today, but I got even by blasting him with my million-volt laser mounted on my roof!" That's alive; that's humor. This was the same event but from a different perspective.

Dramatic embellishment is what children do. That is how we become as children in telling our story. For the perspective of humor is not intended to show disrespect for a story; rather, the intention is to expose the simple beauty of our human clumsiness, the comedy of our human intensity, the blindness that results from focusing too clearly, and the liberation of our spirit when we can see an event in a wider context. "The president's face may be on a dollar, but he is just a small part of God's universe." Humor.

So why these particular bible stories? What is my purpose in sharing them with you? I'm glad you asked.

First of all, these are some of my favorite people in scripture.

Second, they chose me. Their stories shout to me. They wanted to fill in parts of their lives not yet told by writers and preachers. Their "missing pieces" add body to their sketchy, sometimes almost invisible existence in the stories you have heard all your life. And even though they may be supporting cast in the life drama of Christ, they are nonetheless significant in their own dramas. After each story, the main character asks a few questions about *his or her* own life, inviting you to ask parallel questions about *your* story as well. Take some time, preferably the rest of the day, to allow these questions to simmer on a back burner of your mind.

Finally, these are stories to stretch your imagination, to let you see meaning that may have been hidden before, and to help you smile the next time you hear an uninspired sermon about these players of the bible.

Your own story may never be the same.

## Disclaimer

This collection of stories is not about theology, for I work not as a theologian but as a psychotherapist. My work is about people—their struggles, their dilemmas, their sense of family, their political skepticism, their hurts and angers about the unfairness of life. Regularly in my work I use stories from scripture to demonstrate to my clients how much we have in common with the human side of a pharisee, a disciple, a sower of seed, a crazy woman, an executioner.

This bridge that I create is often the first time a bible story becomes relevant to someone in my office or in a lecture room. A man suddenly realizes that he is not just *like* Pilate: he *is* Pilate, caught in a political trap. A woman awakens to the frank reality that she is not just embarrassed by her son's public antics, but that she *is* Mary. It is the human element, the players in the scriptural drama, that holds our attention just long enough for us to hear a lesson. It is in the characters themselves that we see ourselves.

When as a writer or as a counselor I focus on the people in a story, I let them tell their story, often from a viewpoint surprising even to me. And it is their humor, not mine, that I discover and record. Sometimes they are *in* the scene and we see the humore they cannot. At other times the characters are *outside* the scene they had previously experienced, and they see the humore themselves. So, if there is humor, I did not create it; they did! I have simply given them a voice.

# Acknowledgments

This work takes its inspiration largely from sacred scripture. And while I am neither a scripture scholar nor a theologian, I can claim a close friendship with this collection of history, poetry, and revelation. I am indebted to its impact on my life and its companionship in my work.

My wife, Mary Martha, a superb educator and school administrator, a woman of enviable faith and a loving mother, has added a rich dimension to my writing. She has taught me by example that the re-telling of an event is every bit as meaningful and dramatic as the event itself—and certainly more entertaining. I thank her for her encouragement, her literary criticism, and her contribution to preparing this text.

Several people have been encouraging and supportive in this work. Lee Mountain insisted that I persevere because the work needed to be published. Her son, Rocky, warned me to not cross his mother. Fr. Steve Shafran, Rev. Stan Hogle, Rev. Drew Garner, Winnie and Wally Honeywell and Sr. Mary Dennison reviewed the work and offered both helpful comments as to the book's use and some possible and predictable criticisms that would occur as a result of its publication. I am grateful to them for their professional insights and literary comments.

I wish also to thank John Barone, my co-author for the *Leader's Guide*, for his educational and ministerial help as well as his creative involvement in this entire project.

Thank you Jean, Ange, John, and Marty for reading the manuscript and offering insightful corrections.

I wish to thank Billie, Rose, George, Susan, Carol, Paulette, Mr. Alfred Kahn, and all the other waiters and waitresses who have filled my coffee cup and remembered my muffin in restaurants that made this writing possible.

Finally, I wish to recognize the brilliant insight of Mr. Ken Guentert, editorial director of Resource Publications, Inc., to claim this work for review and eventual production.

# Introduction

# *Is This Book for You?*

**Yes, if...**
**...you enjoy reading the bible,** its stories
nibble at your sense of wonder, and you thought
you had exhausted all possible interpretations and
insights into the stories contained therein. Well,
you are in for a delightful surprise; there is humor,
teasing, provocation, and intrigue that you have
yet to discover. After reading this book, your sense
of the sacred might never be the same.
**...you teach in adult religious education,**
and you are constantly in search of contemporary
ways to present scriptural material. You want
stories that don't lose the historical context of the
people and language that gave birth to a
community of believers. You want simplicity,
beauty, and material relevant to real issues of
individuals, couples, and families today. Basically,
you want somebody else to do the work for you.
Look no further.
**...you are a preaching minister** and find that
there are days when even your finest sermon
preparation leaves you, the official inspirer,
uninspired. In desperation you reach for this
volume, read  a story, and suddenly your mind is

flooded with life's little connections with the bible, through you. And you don't even have to quote your source (publisher's rights respected, of course).

**...you're on retreat.** You've kicked back from the hustle and blunders of your normal routine in order to re-focus your life and re-define what's important. The last thing you want to read is a complex, theological, or worse, psychological treatise on someone else's view of what your world should have been had you done it right the first time. No, you want a book that speaks to you from inside the pages of the bible, grabs your imagination, and leaves you thinking, "Thanks. I can use that in my life."

**...you are a church youth minister**. Your job enriches you and exhausts you at the same time. You know better than anyone the cry of the bored teenager: "What does that scripture stuff have to do with us?!" You also know they love stories, especially of impossible situations, love, death, and gossip. They need a challenge; this book will make you look brilliant. The stories can be dramatically performed for liturgical services or classroom. Your imagination is limited only by copyright laws.

**...you struggle with the New Testament**. All your life you have viewed scripture with skepticism; you have difficulty dislodging real people and events from their holy entrapment in God's written word. You have until now chosen the safety of "belief in the bible," which is practiced largely with the bible unopened, unread, and unexamined. More than anything else, you have been fearful of allowing the poetry, letters, books, summaries, and whispers of the bible stir your own creative speculations about these believers who went to work every day, raised families, fought, despaired, and learned—just like you. And like you, they were as skeptical of matters divine then as you are today!

**...you are a serious bible reader.** You, more than anyone else, need this book! You have been stung with any number of religious heresies, which century after century have mistakenly confused "holy" with "beyond," "sacred" with "unapproachable," "respectful" with "serious," "love" with "fear," and "God" with "gone." Every religious group eventually comes to take itself too seriously, largely out of its own fear of disintegration through love—the antithesis of control. And when believers take themselves too seriously, they simultaneously imbue their articles of faith with a seriousness never intended, a seriousness now designed to squeeze out the very life contained in faith.

Watch a professional baseball game. Notice how precisely the rules are followed. Look at the somber faces of the players, the distance of the crowd, the severe scoring, the perfect uniforms, the endless statistics.

Then pay a visit to your neighborhood ballfield and sit for a spell at a young girsl' softball game. See how they smile and laugh and chatter with one another. Watch their excitement both in the dugout and on the field. Observe the intimacy and humor of parents, screaming for a well-hit ball and laughing till they hurt at their children's blunders. And the rules? Who's keeping score? Nobody on the field!

Which scene do you prefer? Better yet, which scene better reflects our divinely human mandate?

To live perfectly and seriously correct, following the rules exactly, risking all on winning over "the opponent," stretched ultimately to be defined as "the evil one"? Or is it to experience our own lives individually and together, loving as we wish to be loved, relishing the brilliance of color rather than obsessing about the price of crayons?

Seriousness is a socially acceptable way to maintain emotional distance. Perhaps serious religion is a way to maintain distance from faith, just as a serious approach to scripture enables us to keep *it* over there, safely disentangled from our real lives over here. Humor is the real enemy, for smiles and laughter and irony and surprise tear away at the boundaries that separate us. Humor bridges gaps, draws us closer, and says for us what cannot be fully translated in language. Humor draws us into the scene in spite of our serious attempts to remain spectators. Humor is not added onto the scene; rather, it is embedded in the profoundly human paradoxes and contradictions in which we find ourselves.

Yet our finest humor is not always immediately apparent. Unlike popular puns and digs and ridicule and slapstick comedy, our most memorable and moving experiences of humor are based on the mind's appreciation of context and the quick twist of meaning in that context.

For example, Jesus, recently celebrated as a popular preacher and healer, is arrested by his political and religious adversaries. He is standing before a civil magistrate, Pilate, who must determine whether there is sufficient evidence to convict Jesus of a punishable crime. Pilate hates his Roman appointment to the Judean wastelands and hates even more the subjects of his jurisdiction, the Jews. He is under close scrutiny by his superiors and desperately wants to eliminate or, better, to prevent any more rebellious uprisings against the power of Rome. Jesus' position is equally well-drawn. He has stirred, in a refreshing way, the hopes and dreams of his people, the oppressed chosen of God. He has openly challenged the hypocritical religious leaders of every community he has visited, and he has called for a revolutionary expression of faith by fulfilling the highest mandate of law: love, rather than condemnation.

There they stand, two men commissioned to enforce the law—one through control, the other through trust and freedom. The *serious* reading of the gospel account is thus:

PILATE: Are you the king of the Jews?

JESUS: Yes, you have said it.

PILATE: This man is innocent of any crime.

Here we have a legal question, followed by a legal admission, followed by a judgment. On to the rest of the historical events. We, the reading audience, observe from the emotional safety of here and now, historical *events* that happened back then and over there. We have a natural resistance to such history, regardless of the degree of respect or reverence we have for the people and the happenings.

Suppose we step into history. Suppose we participate in the *story* that preceded history. Suddenly we are into drama, real people, intense emotion, and personal impact. The present takes over in the movement of story, and it is the present tense that houses the spirit of humor. Now, another not-so-serious historical reading of the gospel account is possible:

Pilate and Jesus face one another. Pilate wants to dismiss this forced legal scene as quickly as possible and has no interest in a formal or lengthy hearing. Jesus, equally disinterested in the rather ridiculous entrapment, has sparred brilliantly in similar face-offs before with countless religious, political, financial, and community leaders of his day. He understands perfectly the dilemma of Pilate and stands with a bemused smile on his face, a smile that has become a hallmark of his provocative, challenging style. Pilate begins with a question to which he and everyone standing around knows the answer—largely because Jesus has openly denied it but nonetheless loves the double meaning continually contained in the question:

PILATE: Are you the king of the Jews?

Jesus opts for the double meaning, while at the same time yielding to political necessity.

JESUS: Whatever you say.

A perfectly staged exchange between an unwilling captor and an unthreatened hostage!

PILATE: Innocent. Case dismissed!

Each has performed his duty in this wonderfully staged trial, while Divine Wisdom is made present in one of the most ironic moments in human history.

*That* is humor. The laughter we experience comes out of that wonderful shift in meaning, that blending of contexts, that clash between the ritualistic obvious and the humanly emotional. Those are the powerfully moving experiences that drive us to exclaim: "You would have to have been there!" And having once experienced this story, then re-reading the historical account is never again the same.

When the Word is made human and is permitted to dwell among us, then can we begin to appreciate the power and beauty of the Word, described in the original meaning of the word "humorous"—alive.

# 1

# *It's the Truth, Mother*

AFTER THIS, JESUS WENT to the other side of the
Sea of Galilee, also called the Sea of Tiberias. A
large crowd kept following him, because they saw
the signs that he was doing for the sick. Jesus went
up the mountain and sat down there with his
disciples. Now the Passover, the festival of the
Jews, was near. When he looked up and saw a
large crowd coming toward him, Jesus said to
Philip, "Where are we to buy bread for these people
to eat?" He said this to test him, for he himself
knew what he was going to do. Philip answered
him, "Six months' wages would not buy enough
bread for each of them to get a little." One of his
disciples, Andrew, Simon Peter's brother, said to
him, "There is a boy here who has five barley
loaves and two fish. But what are they among so
many people?" Jesus said, "Make the people sit
down." Now there was a great deal of grass in the
place; so they sat down, about five thousand in all.
Then Jesus took the loaves, and when he had given
thanks, he distributed them to those who were
seated; so also the fish, as much as they wanted.
When they were satisfied, he told his disciples,
"Gather up the fragments left over, so that nothing
may be lost." So they gathered them up, and from
the fragments of the five barley loaves, left by those
who had eaten, they filled twelve baskets (Jn
6:1-13).

Had it been just a single event, the scene might
have been humorous. There stood nine-year-old
Thomas at the door with a clucking hen tucked
securely under his right arm. Across the room
stood his mother, Sarah, hands on hips, a stern
look on her face. Two other toddlers played in a
corner, oblivious to the family drama.

Sarah was nearing her breaking point with
Thomas. For several weeks now he had been
involved in thefts, in and around their village of
Bethsaida. Always he brought home his bounty:
flour, oil, dried meats, bread. And always he got
caught. Today was no exception.

"It's the truth, Mother," protested Thomas with
great animation. The words "It's the truth" grated
on Sarah's brain like sand on her neck.

"There was this tall rabbi standing...on a rock
wall. He was dressed in black. He said if the hens
were not penned, then I could take them. I only
took one."

"And that's the truth, Thomas Bar Hanna?"
asked his mother sarcastically. She knew there
were no liberated chickens in the neighborhood.
She knew her own words just tightened the spring
on the trap that would soon ensnare her son.

Thomas steeled himself against the power of his
mother's words and the quivering of deceit in his
chest. "You don't believe me, do you?" he almost
shouted. "You don't believe your own son! The hen
is for you, Mother. And you don't even believe me?"

It was moments like this that made Sarah angry
about the death of her husband. She did not want
to be alone to unravel such mental and emotional
knottiness: a child's genuine effort to help his
impoverished family, his remarkable skills at

weaving stories to defend his thefts, her refusal to be duped, and her overriding determination to raise a moral and responsible son. It was all so tiring, so frustrating. And she was not free to back down.

The toddlers, now intrigued by the chicken, were tugging at Thomas' sleeves. Before Sarah could speak, she saw a man appear behind Thomas at the door.

"I want my hen, and I want her now!" boomed their neighbor from up the street. Thomas turned to stone. And without breaking his stare at his mother, he loosened his arm. The hen disappeared backwards into the hands of her owner.

"Sarah, do something about this child, or someone else will!" He turned and was gone.

The stone statue did not move. Sarah, now embarrassed and angry about having been fussed at, struggled to control herself. It was late in the day. She knew she was too tired to deal with the issue adequately.

"I just want to say this for now, Tom," she began. "We don't need to take what is not ours to survive. And telling lies only makes matters worse. If you continue to lie and deceive others, Tom, eventually no one will believe you. And what is worse, you will no longer be able to believe anyone else. Stop it now, before you become so entangled in the net of dishonesty and disbelief that you cannot get out."

The statue bowed his head and shuffled his feet. "I...I..."

"Don't say anything else now!" interrupted Sarah. "It is late. Here." She reached into her apron and drew out two copper coins. "Take these to the merchant and buy what fish and bread you

can for our dinner tonight. And come straight
home."

Thomas came forward and took the coins. Sarah
could see tears in his eyes. He ran for the door,
grabbing their small reed basket on the way out.

Tom could feel a lump in his throat as he ran the
quarter-mile toward the market area of town.
Running always made him feel better; except this
time he could not outrun his mother's words: "You
will no longer be able to believe anyone else." He
promised himself—again—to be truthful. And he
ran.

Nearing the market, he noticed a very large
crowd gathered on a hillside. Though curious, he
continued on because of his mother's presence in
his head and arrived at the merchant. Handing
over the small coins and basket, the merchant
returned to him two dried fish and five loaves of
barley bread. Tom counted them, thanked the man,
and dashed off again toward home. He considered
eating one of the loaves and reporting an exchange
of four loaves and two fish. No. His shame and his
resolution were too fresh.

But his curiosity about the huge crowd was a
different matter. As he arrived at the hill, he could
see someone at the summit gesturing to the people,
and as he drew closer, he noticed everyone silent
and trance-like. Thomas thought that he would
move through the crowd to have a closer look at the
rabbi, hear what he was saying, then hurry home
with the news.

As he knelt on a grassy section of the slope, he
noticed the teacher conferring with two other men.
One of the men came toward Thomas.

"Young man, my name is Andrew. What is yours, and what have you there?"

Thomas nervously responded: "My name is fish, ah, Thomas, uh, and I have two fish and five loaves." Then he quickly added, "And...and they're not mine. They're for my mother and sisters—for dinner. I...I have to go."

"Hold on, hold on please. Don't go yet." The man returned to the rabbi, they exchanged words, then he again approached Thomas.

"Young man," Andrew said, "the teacher over there would like to use your fish and bread."

"What...what for?" asked Thomas.

"Why, to feed these people here who have come to listen and to learn. It is late and..."

Thomas looked around. The entire hill was covered with hundreds of men and women. He thought of ants, then sheep. He looked down into his basket at the two fish and five small loaves. And he heard his mother in his head: "...net of dishonesty and deceit...you can't believe anyone else...."

"You're kidding me, right?" he responded to Andrew. Even Thomas was surprised at his own boldness.

"No, I'm not kidding you. Tell you what: I'll buy your dinner for more than it's worth, and, because you have trusted me, you can still have your dinner back when everyone has been fed."

"Sounds like one of *my* stories!" Thomas let slip. Then Tom looked around again. How could this man be deceiving him with so many onlookers, he thought. And besides, he would have the money to buy food again. The worst that could happen was that he would be fussed at for being late.

"O.K.," agreed Thomas. "But on one condition: I want to go where my basket goes."

"Fine," said Andrew, and he handed the boy three silver coins—ten times the value of the basket's contents.

Thomas was stunned. He handed his basket over and followed the man toward the rabbi who blessed the fish and bread. Then Andrew began to distribute the food to the crowd. Thomas could not believe his eyes. After ten loaves and ten fish had been given away, he grabbed the edge of the basket and looked inside: two fish, five barley loaves. He looked at Andrew, scratched his head, and continued to follow him among the crowd.

After a hundred loaves and a hundred fish were visibly being eaten around him, Thomas looked in his basket again. And again he saw two dried fish and five loaves. "I don't understand, sir."

Andrew paused and said to Thomas, "It is the rabbi: *He* is the one who makes this happen."

The two continued, handing out bread and fish to hundreds of outstretched and grateful hands. Thomas joined in the distribution, each time reaching in and feeling two and five, each time giving away an unending stream of food. It was like nothing he had ever experienced in his life. The ideas of truth and believing began to take on a whole new dimension for him.

Within half an hour an entire mountain of people were dining on dried fish and barley loaves. Then he heard the rabbi instruct the people to gather up the food left uneaten. Baskets appeared, were passed around, filled, and brought to the central area where Thomas stood with Andrew. The boy counted the overfilled baskets outloud: "Two, three,

five, eight, twelve! Twelve, full of fish and bread!"
Impulsively he glanced once more in his own
basket: two fish, five loaves. He had seen it all
unfold before his very eyes. He believed it, and he
couldn't believe he believed it.

"Now, son," said Andrew, "you and your young
friends take these twelve baskets of food home.
They are your reward for believing with a generous
heart. Thank you."

"Thank *you!*" said Thomas excitedly. He started
down the slope carrying two baskets, trailed by
several friends struggling with the remainder.
They walked quickly, laughing and telling and
retelling the unbelievable yet believable event they
had just witnessed. In a rush of shouting and
laughter the boys followed Tom into his home.

There they stood, groaning under the weight of
twelve baskets over-filled with dried fish and
loaves of bread. Sarah stood across the room.

"Mother," gasped Thomas, "there was this tall
rabbi who was standing on a hill, dressed in white.
He said we could have these baskets of food.
It's...it's the truth, Mother."

Sarah fainted.

### Questions I Might Ask Myself

1. When I have repeatedly lied or acted with deceit,
   why do I expect to be believed and trusted when
   I am being truthful?

2. What did Mother mean when she said that the
   great burden of being so deceitful is that the liar
   can't believe anyone else?

3. How can I believe something I don't understand, and how does my growing understanding of life lead me to even more profound beliefs?

# 2

# *Saved from the Jaws of Fame*

THE SCRIBES AND THE Pharisees brought a woman who had been caught in adultery; and making her stand before all of them, they said to him, "Teacher, this woman was caught in the very act of committing adultery. Now in the law Moses commanded us to stone such women. Now what do you say?" They said this to test him, so that they might have some charge to bring against him (Jn 8:3-6).

Yes, I know you, JoAnna."

All action stopped. Before this moment, it would have appeared that everyone milling about the well was either lost in thought or buried in a private conversation with a companion. The hot weather, water problems, the day's chores, family gossip, taxes, foreigners—all topics worthy of debate and complaint. And eavesdropping on someone else's private exchange, while publicly disavowed, remains humankind's favorite pastime.

Especially at a well. For here is where friends and enemies meet through the day, where business is transacted, where counsel is offered and received, where events become news and news becomes the central event. And when a woman with a bad reputation in town is recognized by a popular teacher and preacher—that's news! All other personal and public chatter is suspended as eyes and ears are trained on this unlikely pair.

"Your openness as an equal opportunity lover is widely known in this area," continued the teacher.

Several muffled laughs rippled around the eavesdroppers. JoAnna nervously glanced about. She leaned closer to the teacher, cupped a hand at her mouth, and whispered loudly.

"Highly exaggerated, sir!"

More laughter and sneering nearby.

"I'm sure," replied the teacher. "Hurtful and demeaning gossip usually is. Unfortunately, it makes for such entertaining news that no one bothers to find out whether or not it is true."

"But this woman *is* a tramp!" interrupted a stately voice. A man in noble garb glared at the two. A Sadducee, protector of the Holy Law, was now presiding. "This woman has committed numerous adulterous acts—caught in the act the last time!" Many in the crowd now gathered closer and nodded in agreement at the lawyer's accusation.

The teacher remained seated on the retaining rock wall. He looked up to the man and asked: "And tell us, O dutiful guardian, have you nothing better to do than snoop about and watch with lustful eyes the sexual life of others?!"

The crowd exploded in laughter. Then, surveying the crowd, the teacher added, "And you, busybodies with viper tongues and greedy ears, is this the sort

of garbage you preoccupy your minds with? Is this
what we have come to, that virtue and caring and
love are buried under a manure pile of malicious
gossip and petty backbiting?"

The lawyer stood his ground: "This, sir, is far
from petty. She is a sinful woman and should be
punished! Who are you to make light of such
blatant disrespect of morals, of social values, of the
very commands of Elohim?"

The teacher retorted: "It is true, I am trying to
make light, not of the Law or ethics or morals, but
of the darkness in your minds. And yes, you, sir,
know your law well. Such women—never
men!—are to be stoned to death. So let's get on
with it! We don't need the high court, or due
process, or even witnesses beyond this totally
trustworthy legal giant. And certainly the accused
here, JoAnna, need not plead for her defense, since
by definition she is already discredited. So grab a
stone everyone, large ones please! Let's rid
ourselves of this scandal!"

The crowd stood motionless, looking first to the
teacher, then to the Sadducee, then to JoAnna.
Slowly and deliberately the Sadducee reached
down and picked up a large stone. He looked at the
teacher, then began to toss and catch the rock with
the same hand. He challenged.

"You may mock me, sir, but you will not stop the
will of God or the people's justice from being
executed today."

"So be it, my just one. But I challenge you, and
you, and you, and you," the teacher said to the
crowd."Let anyone who is without sin cast the first
stone."

For a moment no one moved; no one spoke. It was as if they were all frozen in space and time. Then gradually the crowd began to disperse. The Sadducee, seeing his potential support evaporate, tossed down his stone, dusted his hands, and walked away without a word.

The teacher asked,"JoAnna, what has happened to your accusers and your executioners?"

"They have all left, sir."

"Then," said the teacher, "neither shall I accuse you."

"Sir," exclaimed JoAnna, "you have saved my life! Thank you for your strength and compassion and wisdom. I would like to dedicate the remainder of my days traveling from town to town, preaching the dangers of promiscuity, acknowledging my dissolute past, and proclaiming the virtues of marriage and responsible sexuality. I shall lecture to others what I was never willing to be for myself."

The teacher dropped his shoulders and gazed at the sand near his feet. Then looking up into JoAnna's eyes, he sighed.

"JoAnna, we need no more heroes or heroines who take their disgrace on the road for profit. There is, however, something harder—much harder—that you can do."

"What is that, sir?" asked JoAnna excitedly.

The teacher smiled. "It is this: just behave yourself and shut up about it."

## Questions I Might Ask Myself

1. Even when someone else forgives me, why is it so hard to forgive myself?

2. What is my selfish motive in working to save others from the mistakes I've made?

3. What's so difficult about living a responsible and ethical life, and not crowing about it?

4. What would happen if every sinner was punished for every sin and every crime was punished immediately?

5. Why do I want others punished for their wrongdoings but seek compassion for mine?

# 3

# *It Wasn't My Plan*

IN THE SIXTH MONTH the angel Gabriel was sent by
God to a town in Galilee called Nazareth, to a
virgin engaged to a man whose name was Joseph,
of the house of David. The virgin's name was Mary.
And he came to her and said, "Greetings, favored
one! The Lord is with you" (Lk 1:26-29).

Mary had planned to spend the day alone. She
was exhausted from a week of helping her mother
prepare for the birth of an aunt's child, traveling
from town to town, and catching up on work at
home. It was, in fact, pleasurable to be delivering
garments repaired in the family business to people
in their village.

At fifteen, Mary was already looking to the
future. Because of her father's untimely death, her
mother was left to support the family. As the oldest
of three children and quite talented in sewing
skills, Mary had decided to remain unmarried. She
wanted not only to help her aging mother, but she
looked forward to caring for her brother and sister
through her talents. She was clear in her decision
and happy with her choice.

As she approached one of several fountains in the village, she noticed a man drinking. His garment appeared seamless, light in color, and smooth in texture—obviously a well-to-do visitor. He turned to her, lowered his hands from his mouth, and said, "Hello, Mary."

Startled, Mary asked, "Do I know you?"

"No," replied the stranger. "I'm just passing through. Sort of a messenger, you might say."

Mary turned to leave.

"Please, don't go, Mary. Not yet anyway. I've something of importance to say. Please hear me out."

Though shy in nature, Mary nonetheless was taken by the man's appearance and was curious about his knowledge of her.

"What can be so important to say to me?" she asked.

The man smiled and looked firmly into her eyes.

"Mary, you are very special to God, blessed among women. I know that the Spirit of God shall dwell within you. You shall have a son, just as your kinswoman, Elizabeth, is about to have a son. Yours shall be named Jesus, and he shall be a king."

Mary was dazed by the man's words.

"Thank you for the compliment, sir," she replied." But I think you have me confused with some other Mary in our town. Although an engagement has been arranged, I have already decided not to marry. I won't be having a child. My life is dedicated to the family I already have. Good day, sir, whoever you are."

"Mary, wait," he insisted. "Your life is not yours alone to decide. Nobody's is. God has made a plan for you, too."

Annoyed, Mary interrupted. "It isn't *my* plan!"

He continued. "You are not being asked to go against your plan. God is inviting you to stretch your imagination, to think beyond your current sense of duty, and to be open to something grander than your plan. You can still help your family."

"Why me?" she asked. "I'm nobody, an ordinary, hard-working, uneducated girl. Of course I think about a divine plan, but I am not inclined to consider myself any special part of it. So, why me?"

"Why you?" continued the messenger. "Because God prefers to do extraordinary things with quite ordinary people—like yourself. Jesus, your son, will be a king. Some will hear him and follow him *because* he will be ordinary—like them. Others will belittle and reject him for the same reason. What we *are* is no guarantee of either success or failure. All of us, highly ordinary as humans, do the best we can with the talents given us. What impact we really have on one another is beyond our power. We may make a difference. We may not."

Mary was suddenly aware of the weight of the garments she was holding. She lowered them to the ground and knelt beside the pile. The man sat down at the fountain's edge near her. She was lost in thought.

She looked at the man, longer than she knew was polite. She began. "I had it all worked out for myself. A simple life of work with my family. Now I am asked—no, told—to change all that and trust that marriage to Joseph and motherhood are my next steps. It's not easy to let go of what feels right for myself, what I have come to realize is true for me, and consider that someone else's agenda can be at least as valid for me as my own—even if it's God's. I must struggle to somehow make it my plan also if I am to live it honestly and without resentment. I need some time."

The man touched her shoulder reassuringly. "Take some time, Mary. Watch with an open heart and open eyes the events that will be taking place in coming months. Watch as your plan begins to blend with the plan I am describing to you today. Be open to the events that are occurring both inside and outside of you. So that when you finally are able to say 'Thy will be done,' it shall also be your will in concert with God's. I must go now. Peace be with you."

"How will I know that you have spoken the truth to me today?" Mary asked.

Turning to leave, the man replied: "Don't worry about the truth of what I say. Just believe the truth of what is happening to you!"

## Questions I Might Ask Myself

1. How much does "my job" determine who I am? Who would I be without it?

2. Why is it so important to me that events occur *my* way?

3. What do I fear losing by yielding to the plans or will of another?

# 4

# *What Do I Do Now?*

WHEN HE RETURNED TO Capernaum after some
days, it was reported that he was at home. So many
gathered around that there was no longer room for
them, not even in front of the door; and he was
speaking the word to them. Then some people
came, bringing to him a paralyzed man, carried by
four of them. And when they could not bring him to
Jesus because of the crowd, they removed the roof
above him; and after having dug through it, they
let down the mat on which the paralytic lay. When
Jesus saw their faith, he said to the paralytic, "Son,
your sins are forgiven" (Mk 2:1-5).

O h, no!" complained Jacob, as they arrived at the
home of Servius, their cousin. It was already late in
the evening, and it seemed that half the town was
crowded inside and outside the house. "We should
have gotten an earlier start."

"What's wrong?" asked Michael weakly from the
make-shift cot on which he was being carried. "Has
he already left?"

"He's here all right," answered Jacob. "Problem
is, so are a hundred other people packed tighter
than a bale of hay. Standing room only. We can

probably hear him, but I doubt we could get close enough for him to bless you, Michael."

Michael looked up at the darkening blue sky. A few faint stars were appearing, and he began to reflect on how many nights in his life he counted the tiny lights, wondered about their arrangements and questioned their purpose. The stars were his reminder of the questioning he had about his own life: crippled from birth, useless to his family, anticipating a life of beggarly dependence on whoever had the strength and patience to help him. He felt cursed, destined to live in a body that was all but dead.

His one hope for freedom hung on the stories circulating in the area about an itinerant teacher who had a quick mind and a compassionate touch that some said was nothing short of miraculous. He did not want to miss the chance to talk to the visitor and ask for a blessing. But they had arrived too late, and word had it that he would be gone by dawn.

"Okay, Jacob," Michael announced. "If we can't go through the crowd, we'll just fly up to the roof, then swoop down in front of him. Nothing to it."

They chuckled together softly. Then Jacob was struck with creative inspiration.

"Why not!?"

"Why not what?" asked Michael.

"Why not fly up and swoop down?"

"Please, Jacob, it's not really that funny."

Jacob continued, "I'm serious. We could approach Servius' house from the small hill that his roof backs up to, walk across his roof—I mean carry you across—to the covered patio, and lower you down, right beside the master. A little discourteous to Servius, but he'll understand."

Michael felt excitement in his chest, a fluttering of hope again.

"Let's do it. I've nothing to lose, Jacob!"

The gathering of people was spellbound by the words of the teacher. Leaders of the temple and magistrates were questioning his views. Many in pain and with life-long injuries were reaching out for his attention. And no one was the least bit distracted by a man being lowered through the tiled roof onto the ground beside the Nazarean.

Michael felt anxious and exposed as he lay on his cot just a short distance from the man everyone had been talking about. He could see the stars through the roof opening. He could hear words of encouragement, confrontation, and wisdom. The crowd would occasionally laugh, then groan, then sigh, then laugh again. The temple leaders were now challenging the man. Michael was startled when the man's face came between himself and his stars. He was gripped with fear. He felt ashamed.

"Be at peace, my friend," said the face. "Your sins are forgiven."

The crowd murmured around the two. The face disappeared. Stars. Michael was frozen with anticipation.

"Which is easier," continued the absent face, "to forgive sin or to instruct a cripple to walk?"

Michael's heart was pounding in his chest, beads of sweat poured from his brow, and his shoulders trembled. The face returned with a softness and gentleness that steadied every muscle in Michael's body. The face spoke.

"But so that you, my friend, and all those gathered here can know that I speak with the power and authority of our Father who can forgive sin, I say to you: Arise, gather up this pallet, and walk home."

For Michael, time stood still. In this brief instant, he reviewed his entire life of being "the family cripple," an embarrassment to his relatives, a chore for his few and short-lived friendships. He had suffered the humiliation of being a public nuisance, the symbol of some family failure, and despair at being cheated out of a normal life.

Now there were no stars to remind him of his misery. Instead, there was before him a face— inviting, instructing, insisting that he not only let go of his shame, but that he also let go of his entire identity as a cripple! He was being given the opportunity to get off his back and onto his feet, to release his helpers and execute his own walking, to end his first life and begin his second.

Michael could not believe his own mixed feelings about being cured. All his life he had dreamed of a moment like this one. Now it was here, and he found himself reluctant to act on it. Questions flooded his mind.

"What will I do now?"

"Who will know me?"

"Will I know how to walk, to work, to live?"

"Will anyone help me ever again?"

"Will it last?"

"What will I owe this man?"

He reviewed what had just occurred. Two miracles. First, that he was absolved of all guilt and shame. Second, that his lifelong paralysis was gone and that he could walk. Now he was faced with a third challenge. That *he* must do the walking, that from this moment forward he would be forever responsible for his life. The third miracle was up to him and him alone.

Michael saw the face nodding. The man knew what he was thinking! He and the man knew—together—that not even God would do for him what only he could do himself: his own walking. One question remained: now that he could walk, would he?

Impulsively, Michael sat up on one elbow and quickly glanced about. A deadening silence held the onlookers in a trance. A hand reached out to him, then was quickly withdrawn. Someone began to cry. He looked up to the master, and another encouraging nod greeted him.

Michael braced himself on one hand, then reached for a peg protruding from a post that supported the patio. As he pulled his legs and bent them under himself, people began to gasp and groan. Michael reached higher for another peg, drew himself up and stood shakily before the assembly. Cheers and cries erupted. Michael steadied himself and risked a grin. He was on his feet. He turned toward the Nazarean, walked slowly to him, and hugged him tearfully. The congratulations were deafening.

Jacob tapped Michael on the shoulder:
"Hey pal, wanna walk home?"

## Questions I Might Ask Myself

1. Why do I insist on being treated as if I were special?

2. Why is it so difficult to ask for what I need, and why am I so easily upset when others don't already know what I need?

3. When a door of opportunity opens before me, what excuses do I give myself and others for my not walking through it?

4. Whom among those who have helped me in my life have I failed to thank?

# 5

# *Lord, You Must Be Joking!*

THEN SOMEONE CAME TO him and said, "Teacher,
what good deed must I do to have eternal life?" And
he said to him, "Why do you ask me about what is
good? There is only one who is good. If you wish to
enter into life, keep the commandments." He said
to him, "Which ones?" And Jesus said, "You shall
not murder; You shall not commit adultery; You
shall not steal; You shall not bear false witness;
Honor your father and your mother; also, You shall
love your neighbor as yourself." The young man
said to him, "I have kept all these; what do I still
lack?" Jesus said to him, "If you wish to be perfect,
go, sell your possessions, and give the money to the
poor, and you will have treasure in heaven; then
come, follow me." When the young man heard this,
he went away grieving, for he had many
possessions (Mt 19:16-22).

There is nothing like a great dinner to soothe the
spirit—so stands a long-held legend. And a fine
dinner it was: roast goat, fresh potatoes, turnips,
squash, and plenty to drink. Compliments flowed
from guests to host as they continued in avid

discussion of local politics, military movements, and the business opportunities growing in the country.

It was no secret to those at table that one spirit had gone unsoothed by the powers of good food, good drink, good friends, and good talk—the host himself, Rico Nuevo, one of the most successful merchants in the area. His wife and friends had observed him barely eating, slouched heavily beside their table, and sullen to the point of being barely present to the congenial gathering. Hoping to draw him out, his longtime friend, Benjamin, risked impoliteness.

"And now a toast for our host, a man who is most like the goat that was roast."

Cheers and laughter filled the room. Even Rico could not refrain from a smile, then a friendly sneer, toward Benjamin.

"Come on now, Ric," said Benjamin. "What's weighing so heavily on your chest this lovely evening?"

"Yes," added his wife, Sylvia, "you've been doing your limp towel routine all day, and you haven't spoken a word about your gloom with me. Your friends are here; maybe they can drag it out of you."

"Speak up, ol' man," encouraged Joshua. "We won't eat you; we're full already."

More laughter and friendly banter crisscrossed their table.

"It's nothing," responded Rico. "Or, at least it ought to be nothing, but something about everything..."

Everyone glanced shyly about the room, shoulders shrugged, palms up.

"Ah ha!" exclaimed Benjamin. "A riddle! I love riddles. Nothing that's something about everything. Ummm."

"I've got it!" shouted Jonas. "An empty purse!" More laughter.

"No, no, no," shrugged Rico. "I mean the teacher. Something he said. Obviously, you've all heard of him. I spoke with him today. Interesting fellow."

"Go on, go on," urged Sylvia.

"You sure you all want to hear this?"

Jonas chuckled. "Sir, this is your house, your food; we are your guests, and your sweet wife will bury her nails in your arm if you don't. Do you need more convincing?"

"Well said, Jonas!" exclaimed Benjamin.

Rico placed his cup before him and fingered its ornate design as he continued. "He...the teacher... was in the vicinity earlier today. He was preaching about life after death, the love of God, the goodness of being poor. These thoughts were not exactly foreign to me. My servant and I stood and listened, and I decided to challenge him with a question, only half seriously, of course."

He paused and looked around the table at everyone's attentive face.

"I asked him what I had to do to gain eternal life—if there *is* life after death. Then he challenged me by asking what the scriptures already say."

Jonas interrupted: "Yes, the teacher is fast on his feet. I've heard him myself."

"So I recited for him and the onlooking crowd," continued Rico,"what is in the scripture."

"What did you answer?" asked Benjamin.

"That we are to love God fully and our neighbors likewise."

34

"Excellent!" applauded the guests.

"But he said, 'Then do it.' To which I responded, 'I already do.'"

"I can vouch for that, Ric!" exclaimed Simeon. "For a man of wealth, you possess the disgusting quality of also being decent!"

The group laughed in agreement.

"Go on," invited Sylvia.

"Well, he said that there was one thing else I must do then, to...to sell all that I have, give it to the street people, and follow him."

A deafening silence filled the dining room. Minds were racing. Puzzlement was evident on several faces. Finally Jonas said, "Surely he meant it in humor."

Rico looked at his friend. "That's exactly what I thought. So I asked him, 'Lord, you must be joking?!' He didn't respond. He just looked at me, daring me to figure it out on my own. We left."

"The man's a lunatic!" said Thadius. "I've heard similar nonsense. We all know that good fortune, even wealth, is a sign of God's approval and blessing. How then can a man be expected to reject God's blessing by choosing to be poor? Absurd!"

"I've heard him myself," added Jonas. "He says the poor are blessed and that the rich are in trouble. He's got it backwards, if I do say so!"

"That's what's bothering me," said Rico. "If obeying the Law of God and loving others is not hard enough, he adds that earning an eternal reward demands becoming destitute. It just doesn't make sense. I'm willing to do what is right and just. I'm not opposed to fairness and kindness. But my very lifestyle, my hard-earned income, my position of financial security and productivity? I've always been responsible and earned what I got. Can he be serious that such a price must be paid for salvation?"

"The Nazarene is himself poor," said Thadius. "He was born indigent, has no job history, and lives off charity. Of course he preaches the virtue of poverty. What would be his attitude were he of wealth?"

"Which is the point," said Sylvia. "There are no rich prophets. You can be as bold as he only if you've nothing to lose!"

The group laughed heartily and toasted Sylvia.

"Which is *my* point!" shouted Rico. "If you have nothing, how then can you earn eternal life?"

The group went silent, then grumbled noisily its inability to respond to Rico's question. Suddenly their gaze was directed to a young child entering in night clothes and approaching their host. Rico softened and smiled as he opened his arms to his daughter.

"Come in, honey," he said. "What do I have to do to get a good night kiss from Jessica?"

"Wrong question, Papa," she answered as she was lifted onto Rico's lap.

"Wrong question? What do you mean, darling?"

Jessica responded. "Papa, you don't have to do nothing to get my kisses. They are free, just because I love you."

She kissed her father, slid from his lap and proceeded out of the room. Rico's face was pale. Tears trickled from his eyes. And no one could speak.

## Questions I Might Ask Myself

1. Why do I feel I have to earn whatever I get?

2. Why is the gift of love so difficult to accept?

3. To what extent must I control the world around me by keeping people indebted to me or afraid of me?

# 6

# *I Don't Understand*

NOW THE BIRTH OF Jesus the Messiah took place in
this way. When his mother Mary had been engaged
to Joseph, but before they lived together, she was
found to be with child through the Holy Spirit. Her
husband Joseph, being a righteous man and
unwilling to expose her to public disgrace, planned
to dismiss her quietly. But just when he had
resolved to do this, an angel of the Lord appeared
to him in a dream and said, "Joseph, son of David,
do not be afraid to take Mary as your wife, for the
child conceived in her is from the Holy Spirit. She
will bear a son, and you are to name him Jesus, for
he will save his people from their sins." All this
took place to fulfill what had been spoken by the
Lord through the prophet:

> "Look, the virgin shall conceive and bear a son,
>     and they shall name him Emmanuel,"

which means "God is with us." When Joseph awoke
from sleep, he did as the angel of the Lord
commanded him; he took her as his wife... (Mt
1:18-24).

J oseph awoke with a start. He sat up, swung his
feet to the dirt floor beneath his straw bed and

groaned as he buried his face in his hands. His head was throbbing, as if inhabited by voices other than his own.

Snap! The dream. There was another voice. Slowly it began to unravel. An instruction, spoken with authority and reassurance that he was not supposed to question his beloved's mysterious pregnancy, that he was to disregard public embarrassment and family disapproval, and that he should proceed with their marriage as if he himself had directed the entire series of events.

Confusion flooded Joseph's mind.

"I just don't understand!" he heard himself shout. He quickly glanced about his small apartment, impulsively checking that he was alone, lest he be seen behaving as a lunatic. He was alone.

"I did not ask that you understand," a voice announced.

Joseph leapt from his bed and again surveyed the room. Fear began to join his confusion as he realized that either he was not alone or he was going crazy. He bolted for the door, flung it open and stepped out into the dark and chilly morning, desperately hoping to see a friend or neighbor there joking with his groggy mind. No one.

He turned, walked slowly back inside and decided to risk total insanity.

"Who is here?"

His eyes darted back and forth, his heart pounding. He cautiously sat on the edge of his bed.

"Relax, Joseph," came a reply. "I'm the same voice who spoke to you in your sleep. I have returned mainly so that you will know I have indeed been with you this past night."

"I don't understand," Joseph softly responded.

"That's the second reason I am speaking to you again. You're not understanding," said the voice. "You are a good, responsible, and loving person, Joseph. And you work hard to make sense of what is occurring in your life. But I must caution you, life is such that you do not always have the opportunity, skill, or luxury to understand before you act. There are times when you are called on to trust your heart, your intuition, or the demands of the moment. Insisting that you must understand before you proceed can be nothing short of disaster at worst, and missed opportunity at best.

"This is one of those moments, Joseph. You are this day being urged to act on your and Mary's behalf, without wavering about consequences or public opinion."

Joseph couldn't help himself. It just slipped out. "I...I don't understand."

"Precisely," said the voice, matter-of-factly. "You do not understand today. You may gain some understanding as the years go by, and you likely will never fully understand the implications of this invitation in your brief lifetime.

"You see, Joseph, no one ever understands sufficiently the course of one's life. We put a few pieces of information together in order to make some livable sense out of it, but we delude ourselves into thinking we understand it. Understanding is about having some perspective on things, and perspective is the one thing denied us in our own lives. To live fully *in* your life is to be willing to forego understanding, and to trust in something more available, and more profound."

Joseph now found himself eager to follow.

"And what is that?" he asked.

"You must be willing to take such full responsibility for your life that you are prepared to answer to anyone without apology. You must have such faith in yourself and your willingness to push on that you do not question the judgments you make today with the information available to you. It is faith in your own goodness and integrity, Joseph—not understanding. For, most of the time, sufficient information is not available. To wait for that is to wait out your lifetime and to doubt your every move!"

"Like I've been doing these past days," affirmed Joseph.

"Exactly," reaffirmed the voice. "Thus, my mission. Now, it's in your hands. And, by the way, Joseph, you do good work with your hands."

Joseph smiled: "*That* I can understand."

## Questions I Might Ask Myself

1. Everyone hears voices inside. What can I do to better listen to this internal dialogue and use the information contained in it?

2. Why do I so easily avoid or reject what I do not immediately understand?

3. What can I do to stay open to learning and to believing without becoming overly skeptical?

# 7

# *Panicky Pigs*

THEY CAME TO THE other side of the sea, to the
country of the Gerasene. And when he had stepped
out of the boat, immediately a man out of the tombs
with an unclean spirit met him. He lived among
the tombs; and no one could restrain him any more,
even with a chain; for he had often been restrained
with shackles and chains, but the chains he
wrenched apart, and the shackles he broke in
pieces; and no one had the strength to subdue him.
Night and day among the tombs and on the
mountains he was always howling and bruising
himself with stones. When he saw Jesus from a
distance, he ran and bowed down before him; and
he shouted at the top of his voice, "What have you
to do with me, Jesus, Son of the Most High God? I
adjure you by God, do not torment me!" For he had
said to him, "Come out of the man, you unclean
spirit!" Then Jesus asked him, "What is your
name?" He replied, "My name is Legion; for we are
many." He begged him earnestly not to send them
out of the country. Now there on the hillside a
great herd of swine was feeding; and the unclean
spirits begged him, "Send us into the swine; let us
enter them." So he gave them permission. And the
unclean spirits came out and entered the swine;
and the herd, numbering about two thousand,
rushed down the steep bank into the sea, and were
drowned in the sea (Mk 5:1-13).

The village of Kersa considered itself fortunate. Nestled on the east bank of Lake Tiberias, it lay just outside the bickering Judean states and was able to maintain its historic Greek character. It was a quiet, pastoral community, largely excluded from regional events. In effect, nothing much ever happened in Kersa.

Until earlier this morning when the stranger arrived. By mid-day, the town was in a frenzy. Some forty to fifty herdsmen had gathered at the magistrate's court, along with some of their wives and children, and a few craftsmen. Accounts of the morning's events were being shared, compared, and argued. The noise was gradually reaching a deafening pitch when Sophia, wife of the resident judge, appeared through the door.

A hush fell over the gathering. They waited.

"Welcome to our courtyard, gentlemen," beamed Sophia. "Can I be of some service to you?"

Joakim, a respected herdsmen, was standing in front of the group. He glanced about, and stepped forward.

"We need to speak to your husband, Travelia. We have a matter of great urgency to present to him."

The crowd shouted in agreement. Sophia raised her hand for silence.

"He is currently in Samaria and should return in two days. I am available to hear your concern, have our scribe record the details, and invite you to reconvene on his return. So please, calm yourselves and let us talk."

As an attendant brought out a chair for Sophia, the men busily debated the pros and cons of dealing with the magistrate's wife. They concluded it to be an unusual but workable situation. Sophia had frequently accompanied her husband in matters of business and judgment. The townspeople respected her as much as her spouse.

A consensus was reached. Men began to shout:

"I lost twenty five!"

"I lost forty!"

"What about my fifteen?!"

"And my sixty?!"

Sophia raised her hand. "Gentlemen! Please! Let's start at the beginning. Can someone speak of the morning's events? Joakim, tell me. What is this all about?"

Joakim gripped his cloak with both hands and cleared his throat: "Madame...we...I mean I...and we were gathering our swine herds for trade near the shore at about the third hour. The area is lined with caves used for burying our dead. And as is well-known, a man named Delirius, possessed by demons, lives among the caves."

"Yes, we all know Delirius, a pitiful man," said Sophia. "Please continue."

Joakim's voice began to rise. "Well, there we are with our herds when a boat lands at lakeside and several men disembark. Delirius rushes from a cave nearby, screams at them, and one of the strangers screams back. Suddenly Delirius turns toward us, hurls himself stark naked into the middle of our herds, stampedes the pigs, and they all perish among the rocks in the water."

"Most devilish thing I ever saw!" shouted another herdsman.

"And we want our pigs back!" screamed another.

The crowd joined in with insults and accusations. Sophia raised her hand. "Gentlemen! Let me see if I have this straight for our scribe. A stranger

confronts a local madman who exposes himself to
your pigs that commit suicide in the lake."

Joakim hurriedly responded: "Not exactly,
madame, with due respect, of course. The stranger
challenged the demons that somehow entered the
swine and caused their death."

"Yes, yes, that's it," confirmed another.

"Alright, alright," said Sophia. "I think I
understand now. A bunch of devils were snatched
from Delirius and hurled into the pigs who were
hurled into the water—all done by the stranger."

"Yes, yes, that's how it happened!" shouted the
now-excited herdsmen.

"And you say you want your pigs back—
possessed and drowned?" inquired Sophia, holding
back an inopportune laugh.

"Not exactly, madame, with due respect, of
course," replied Joakim. "We would like you...uh...
or Travelia to see to it that someone makes good
our loss."

"And how many pigs are we talking about, good
sir," asked Sophia.

The men shouted out in chorus.

"Eighty!"

"Three hundred!"

"Two thousand!"

"Liars!" a voice bellowed over the crowd.
Herdsmen, children and women turned and gasped
at the sight of Delirius, standing at the gateway.
He was bathed, dressed, and groomed. A serenity
about him was tinged with firmness in his voice.

"You are all trying to make a fool of Sophia, just
as you have long made a fool of me at the caves."

"You must be Delirius," interrupted Sophia.

"I am. And for years I have been cursed by the demons of ridicule, poverty, rejection, abuse, and disgrace. I have been treated by these pigs as if I were an animal. Their greed, that robbed me of my life, is now directed toward you, Sophia."

The men shouted threats and waved their fists.

"And the stranger?" asked Sophia. "What of him?"

Delirius stepped forward. "He dared me to be the man I once was; he challenged the demons I kept hidden inside, and I found myself screaming with joy and freedom."

Sophia turned toward Joakim.

"And now I ask you, sir, a man respected in this village: how many pigs panicked and drowned in the excitement and confusion? The *truth*, Joakim!"

And indeed it was a moment of truth for Joakim. His friends on one side, his accuser on the other, his judge before him.

"Well...uh...the number? I would say, madame, that the number was...was...eleven."

The crowd grumbled. Sophia raised her hand for silence.

"And you, Delirius. Tell us how many swine were stolen from you by these thieves."

"Madam," responded Delirius, "the number stolen from me six years ago was eleven!"

The crowd burst into argumentative clamor.

Sophia then announced:

"Since there is no dispute as to the facts, it seems as though the stranger has already satisfied justice. I for my part shall recommend to my husband, your magistrate, that he enjoin each of you herdsmen to compensate Delirius with one pig each for his loss over these six years. *And* be sure that the animal you hand over to this man be, unlike yourselves, a *healthy* swine! Now, get on with your day."

As the crowd began to file out of the courtyard, Delirius signaled for Joakim to step aside.

"Joakim," he said, "thank you for speaking the truth."

"How could I do otherwise, Delirius? I was surrounded. But what about out there in the countryside. Will the truth ever be told?"

"My friend," said Delirius, "each man here today knows the truth. That alone matters."

Sophia watched them leave together.

## Questions I Might Ask Myself

1. What demeaning and prejudiced labels do I apply to people so that I can write them off as less than I?

2. Why do I have difficulty remaining truthful and fair when called upon to assess financial loss, as with an insurance claim?

3. When I am caught in a lie, what prevents me from being truthful? Why do I persist in the lie?

# 8

# *Blessed Are the Righteous*

THEN THE LORD SAID to him: "Now you Pharisees clean the outside of the cup and the dish, but inside you are full of greed and wickedness. You fools! Did not the one who made the outside make the inside also? So give for alms those things that are within; and see, everything will be clean for you.

"But woe to you Pharisees! For you tithe mint and rue and herbs of all kinds, and neglect justice and the love of God; it is these you ought to have practiced, without neglecting the others. Woe to you Pharisees! For you love to have the seat of honor in the synagogues and and to be greeted with respect in the marketplaces. Woe to you! For you are like unmarked graves, and people walk over them without realizing it" (Lk 11:39-44).

REPORTER: Good evening, ladies and gentlemen. Tonight on Spotlight we have with us someone you have all met before, a prominent leader of our community. Mr. Righteous Etticus, a ranking Pharisee. Welcome, Mr. Etticus. May I call you Righteous?

RIGHTEOUS: I don't think that would be right. Since this is our first meeting, I think Mr. Etticus is the proper form.

REPORTER: Of course, of course. Now, Righteous—I mean, Mr. Etticus—tell us something about your work as a Pharisee.

RIGHTEOUS: I must correct you here, for my high position is not work per se. Rather it is my life. I am profoundly dedicated to the awesome task of pharisaical zeal. I am, in a word, the defender of our faith that is enshrined in Law and lived out through strict compliance with that Law in daily life.

REPORTER: How interesting, Etticus. So you must be both an expert in the Law as well as an enforcer of it.

RIGHTEOUS: Not exactly. True, I am eminently versed in the Law, highly trained in its details of application, and licensed to teach it. And while I may be viewed by the less-informed as an enforcer, that title is harsher than I prefer to define my vocation. I am more a visible voice of conscience than a member of a police force.

REPORTER: A brilliant distinction!

RIGHTEOUS: More than brilliant, my good man. A necessary one.

REPORTER: So tell us, Etticus, how do you do your job...er...work...er...

RIGHTEOUS: Task. I am among a privileged few who are commissioned by God to regularly inform one and all—without exception—how they should behave in every category of life. I must alert people when they are wrong, inappropriate, misinformed, out of line, and immoral. I am ever vigilant to what is being done, how it is performed, timing, motivation, circumstance, and, of course, who is doing a deed. Nothing escapes my monitoring skills; everything comes under my scrutiny.

REPORTER: Sounds as though being a hard-line Pharisee is no easy life. But aren't you taking a rather extreme position in the long and rich tradition of rabbinical Judaism? My understanding is that there has been a wide range of discussion, debate, and even compassion in the application of the Law by the Pharisees of history. Aren't you a bit to "the right," so to speak, in your posture, Mr. Righteous?

RIGHTEOUS: Mr. Etticus. Not from where I see it, young man. Somebody has to draw the line. Somewhere debate must yield to action, to the rules of the game—the right rules. That is my duty. There is also reward. For the importance of my position is enhanced by the fact that each time I inform someone that he (or she) is not allowed to behave that way; each time I avoid the unclean, the unfaithful, the immoral, and the ignorant; each time I perform a public ritual perfectly—then I am rewarded with the immediate approval of God and I have earned my entrance into eternal life.

REPORTER: Wow! You really are important! Without your supervisory viewpoint and your divinely commissioned duty to confront and correct the misguided souls of the world, then we wouldn't have a snowball's chance in Gehenna to get on the right track for salvation.

RIGHTEOUS: Not so fast. I didn't say that my task was to help save souls. I said earlier that my task was to protect the integrity of the Law. What the unclean and ignorant among us do with their lives or their salvation is largely out of my jurisdiction. I let them know that they are wrong and that I am right. My approval is guaranteed, theirs is highly questionable. I am important and highly regarded because I am a living example—a model—of what Law-abiding should be. The better I look, and the worse they feel, then the more perfectly I have fulfilled my calling.

REPORTER: So we might conclude, Righteous Etticus, far right Pharisee, that the worse the general populace feels about themselves, then the greater evidence you have that you have done well and are indeed deserving of an eternal reward.

RIGHTEOUS: Heavens no, clumsy sir! You, like others before you, have erroneously concluded that we lord it over the less fortunate, or that we parade about with arrogant pride in our positions as holy protectors, or that we are condescending to the lowly and dirty of the earth. We righteous ones simply and zealously point out the flaws in others—their failure to comply with the Law. Someone has to do it. Are we to be criticized for performing this on-going task of public legal purification?

REPORTER: I should say not! You are certainly to be admired and respected for your efforts. However, someone has just handed me a note with a question I would welcome your thoughts on. Has your brilliance in being right and the lowly being wrong ever inspired even a single soul to hope for God's approval or joy in life?

RIGHTEOUS: I would answer that the question is poorly constructed and based on a false premise. You see, goodness and joy flow from obedience to Law. The questioner should have asked, "Why are we still unhappy when in fact we do what is expected of us?"

REPORTER: Yes. Can you answer the improved question?

RIGHTEOUS: Of course I can! Your questioning of my competence is itself disrespectful and annoying!

REPORTER: I'm sorry. I didn't mean to imply...

RIGHTEOUS: Regardless! If someone is complying with the Law and finds himself still unhappy, then he is obviously without God's approval and is therefore incapable of fully complying with the Law.

REPORTER: Somewhat of a hopeless circle, wouldn't you say, your Exactness?

RIGHTEOUS: I don't *make* the Law. I only enforce—I mean, protect—the Law.

REPORTER: And are *you* happy?

RIGHTEOUS: What kind of a question is that? I don't have to be happy! What I do is serious

work! This is my life! I don't need to be happy! I
have something greater than happiness! I have
the privilege of being right! No one may like me
and I may be miserable, but by God, *I am right!*

REPORTER: Thank you, thank you so much,
Righteous Etticus, extremist legal eagle at large,
for this most inspiring discussion. And now, back
to our regularly scheduled program.

## Questions I Might Ask Myself

1. Have I ever seriously examined why I fight so
much to be right?

2. Have I noticed how quickly I push people away—
even those I love— by making every issue one of
who's right?

3. Is God flattered by my crushing of people around
me when I use His Word to demean and
humiliate them?

# 9

# *On the Way to a Party*

THEN THE KINGDOM OF heaven will be like this. Ten
bridesmaids took their lamps and went to meet the
bridegroom. Five of them were foolish, and five
were wise. When the foolish took their lamps, they
took no oil with them; but the wise took flasks of oil
with their lamps. As the bridegroom was delayed,
all of them became drowsy and slept. But at
midnight there was a shout, "Look! Here is the
bridegroom! Come out to meet him!" Then all those
bridesmaids got up and trimmed their lamps. The
foolish said to the wise, "Give us some of your oil,
for our lamps are going out." But the wise replied,
"No! there will not be enough for you and for us;
you had better go to the dealers and buy some for
yourselves." And while they went to buy it, the
bridegroom came, and those who were ready went
with him into the wedding banquet; and the door
was shut. Later the other bridesmaids came also,
saying, "Lord, lord, open to us." But he replied,
"Truly I tell you, I do not know you." Keep awake
therefore, for you know neither the day nor the
hour (Mt 25:1-13).

Okay! Okay! Don't break the door down!" The
small shop echoed with more banging mingled with
excited voices.

"I'm coming! I'm coming!" shouted Petrolius as he made his way through the darkness of the apartment and into his adjoining shop. A single lamp was continually lit there—his personal statement that he was always available for business. Nonetheless, in these his later years, getting up in the middle of the night was less and less worth the effort to him.

"Why can't people show up during the day to buy lamp oil?" he mumbled to himself. Then quickly added, "And why did I ever think it was such a good idea to be available night and day to this town?"

He unlatched the door, swung it half open and peered drowsily into the five faces that smiled at him.

"Teenagers!" he thought to himself.

"Whatta you young ladies want? It's past midnight! Whatta you doing out on the streets at this time of night?"

The five giggled to one another, covering their mouths, shuffling their feet, pushing and jabbing each other, voting for who would speak for the band of night visitors. Virginia was elected.

"Sir, we are on our way to a wedding, and..."

"A wedding?" shot back Petrolius. "In the middle of the night? I've no time for jokes, girls, especially when I should be sleeping. Run along and play somewhere else!" He slammed the door. "Teenagers!"

"Please, Petrolius, please!" came the cries through the door. Now the mood of the voices was one of panic rather than play. "Please, sir, let us explain!"

The door opened. A momentary silence.

"Okay, explain," challenged the old man.

Virginia began again: "Sir, we are members of a wedding party, the wedding of Tardion the shepherd. Surely you know his family."

"Yes, yes," responded Petrolius impatiently. "I know of the marriage. But I heard the wedding was called off because of marauding thieves spotted in the hills nearby."

"We were told to wait for his return," said Virginia. "He did return—late—and it was decided to go on with the celebration."

"So why aren't you there, instead of roaming the streets at this late hour?"

"Because, sir, some of us ran out of lamp oil, while others went on ahead in attendance. You're the only dealer in town. So we hurried here to get oil."

The four others nodded in agreement with Virginia's story.

Petrolius studied the young ladies' faces, motioned for them to enter, and led them to a central table. The girls stood silently as Petrolius turned and asked, "But why didn't you fill your lamps when you started out?" Even as the words were leaving his mouth, he realized that he must have asked this or similar questions a thousand times in his life. Why people didn't check their lamps, be prepared for the unexpected, or plan ahead was a never-ending wonderment for him. Why was it so common for folks to take initiative only when their backs were against the wall, rarely before? Why did they expect that someone would bail them out of trouble, that they somehow deserved to be rescued when they had gotten themselves in a pickle by being negligent or thoughtless or sloppy?

He knew even before she answered that Virginia would plead ignorance and blame her and her companions' dilemma on someone else.

"We didn't know the groom would take so long," she responded. "This has never happened before to any of us. We thought the other women would help us, but to our surprise, they refused. So we ran all the way to your shop. And if you keep asking so many questions, you're going to make us late and we won't be allowed in."

The smile on Petrolius' face revealed an almost toothless mouth. He loved being right.

"Does our plight strike you as humorous, sir?" sneered another of the five.

"No," reassured Petrolius as he shook his head. "It's just too complicated to explain to you. Now, who's paying for the lamp oil?"

The five looked at one another in puzzlement, then to the shopkeeper. "Sir," pleaded one, "we forgot about money. We were in such a rush..."

Petrolius laughed. "I'm not believing this! You kids are a walking disaster! And before the night is over, you'll conclude that you missed the party because everyone else—including me—failed to cooperate in your evening plans. You girls have a lot to learn about the real world!"

"Perhaps you are right," said Virginia, "but I doubt that you were as wise at sixteen as you are today."

"Not bad, not bad at all, young lady. Here, take some oil and get out of here. You need to play, and I need to rest."

The five accepted the gift, thanked the old merchant, and hurried into the darkness. Petrolius closed the door and grumped: "Teenagers!"

## Questions I Might Ask Myself

1. Why does the world have so much trouble complying with *my* schedule?

2. What can I do to help others understand my timing and my plans?

3. How do I respond or react to disruptions in my day, and how do I make allowances for others' schedules?

# 10

# *Prison*

FOR HEROD HIMSELF HAD sent men who arrested
John, bound him, and put him in prison on account
of Herodias, his brother Philip's wife, because
Herod had married her. For John had been telling
Herod, "It is not lawful for you to have your
brother's wife." And Herodias had a grudge against
him, and wanted to kill him. But she could not, for
Herod feared John, knowing that he was a
righteous and holy man, and he protected him.
When he heard him, he was greatly perplexed; and
yet he liked to listen to him (Mk 6:17-20).

Why anyone would light a torch in broad
daylight surprised Janus as he stood waiting
outside the only prison in the entire region. The
building was smaller than he had imagined, no
bigger than a family home or a stable. And while
there were no windows visible to the front, he
assured himself that some existed in the rear.

He stepped back as the dwarf-sized jailer
fumbled with the latch, cursed, then struggled to
open a door that could just as easily have fallen off
its single leather hinge. A prison with hardly a

door, tended by a wretch who could barely get in—
the whole scene made Janus chuckle to himself.

"Mind your feet, Sir Scribe!" ordered the little
man. "These steps are three hundred years old and
break many an ankle. Mind your feet."

The two began descending a stairway carved out
of limestone, winding down into an ever-darkening
chamber. Now the torch needed no explanation, as
it revealed huge cracks in the almost circular wall,
uninhabited spider webs, and the rounded edges of
steps worn smooth by countless criminals, guards,
and occasional visitors like himself.

Janus reminded himself, with relief, that he was
just a visitor, doing his job. The odor of stale urine
and feces rushed up to meet him as his head jerked
with repulsion. He wondered why he had not
anticipated such a shock. Not a sound could be
heard except for the scraping of their boots down
the steps.

As they arrived at a stone floor caked with dried
mud and straw, the jailer hoisted his torch to a
wall hook, turned, and began to ascend the steps.
Janus impulsively grabbed his arm and heard
himself almost pleading.

"Wait! Where are you going?"

The little man jerked his arm free and without so
much as a glance toward his visitor replied, "Up.
When you're done, bring the torch." He continued
up with a labored climb, while Janus followed him
with his eyes for several moments. He would have
preferred to have company in this hole.

Janus glanced around, and seeing no one,
retrieved the torch from the wall. He cautiously
stepped along the perimeter of the dungeon, circled

it back to the stairway, then stiffened with surprise as he saw a pair of legs behind the steps.

"The Baptist? " inquired Janus. Silence. "I...I am Janus, Scribe and Lawyer in the service of..."

"I know, I know!" shot back a stern and rough voice from the darkness. "One of Herod's jackals. Come to dine on human bones?"

Janus moved closer, crouched against the wall, and sat his torch beside him. His stomach tightened as he viewed the frightening face before him: dirty, gaunt, wild eyes, matted hair on head and jaw, cracked lips. This was the same man he had watched and listened to from afar many times. Yet it was not the same man. The two images would not come together in his mind. Janus began again.

"John, no one knows I'm here—not even Herod, though he likely would not object. Here, I've brought you something."

Janus reached into his purse and pulled out two strips of dried goat meat. He held them out to the prisoner and for the first time noticed his own hand trembling.

Chains rattled as John leaned forward and, reaching for the meat, grabbed Janus' wrist instead. Janus gasped.

"Frightened, my angel of mercy?" sneered John.

The two men glared at one another.

"Yes," said Janus. "I don't like being here."

John released him and slowly took the meat strips from his hand.

"Aren't you afraid it may be poisoned?" asked Janus.

"Why?" shrieked John. "I'm a dead man already. I'll either starve to death here or be executed out

there. You know the routine, Janus. You're the
legal expert; your master, whose hand holds the
other end of *your* chain, has probably already
decided."

"You never let up, do you, John?" snapped Janus
as his jaw tightened and anger began to boil inside
his neck. "No one owns me!"

"Don't insult me with your self-deceit, Scribe.
You lawyers prostitute yourselves to the highest
bidder, then justify your greed by calling it service
to the Law. You've sold yourself to Herod. He
yanks your chain—silver though it may be."

"And you, John, who have you sold your soul to?
Elohim? The Nazarene? Your own fame? You have
the arrogance of an elephant, trampling on
whosoever's toes you choose. People say you're
trying to be Elijah, a re-make of a dead prophet."

John took a bite of the goat strip, chewed it
slowly and deliberately, savoring its richness. He
grinned. "And who do you think I am, learned one?"

"I think you are a zealot gone mad. I think you're
self-destructive. I think you went too far when you
embarrassed Herod about his remarriage.
And...and I don't want you to die."

"Why not? Surely you can help your owner
contrive a socially acceptable explanation for
ending my life."

"John, you know even better than I that *how* you
say something is every bit as important as what
you say. Which, by the way, is why I'm here. I
admire you. In many ways you are a better
spokesman for our faith than the priests and
ministers selected for that task. But you will die if
you don't retract what you said about Herod
marrying his ex-sister-in-law. So what? Who cares?

Herod's personal life is of no importance to anyone but..."

"God?" interrupted John. "I have no personal issue with Herod. He is irrelevant to me, except that he too has lost his way. I have not condemned the man. He has condemned himself with his disregard for the Law, propriety, decency, and the position of authority he has among his people. Retracting my words will not change his failure as a leader. He will kill me for speaking what is unspeakable. It is the messenger who pays with his life for the message he brings. The perpetrator of the evil is allowed to live; his lawyers see to that!"

Janus studied the face of John. His fear was gone; he wanted to be here. All the news about the Baptist came crashing in on him with stunning accuracy, and he wished that he had met and talked with John earlier in his life.

John studied the face of his visitor and saw in his eyes a spirit strong, searching, yearning for a freedom he could not find. And in a brief flash of awareness, John realized that while many in his own life had admired and feared him, this man, Janus, loved him. Janus broke the silence.

"You are correct John: we are much alike. You speak on behalf of the Nazarene; I, on behalf of Herod. We are each caught up in a drama and destiny larger than ourselves. And we shall both die, knowing that we were never masters of our own fates. And for what?"

"For the one thing," replied John, "that gives life meaning, my friend."

"And what is that?"

"That we act our parts well, that we be exactly who we are—fully, passionately, and as lovingly as we can be in this brief life given to us. Our destiny is to become who we are. Our only sin is to wish to be what we are not."

"I don't understand," said Janus.

John continued. "Men and women long for the past, dream of what might be, pretend to be someone else, and deny responsibility for their own deeds. They wait to be led like nameless sheep, hide from opportunities, blame the conditions of life and the bad will of others, and blend into someone else's life for safety and approval. All this to avoid the terrible risk of finding out that our own, unique lives are the *only* thing we can claim when we die."

Janus hesitated, then asked, "Do we ever know for sure?"

"That!" exclaimed John, "is the humor of God."

In a lighted prison, two brothers smiled at one another.

## Questions I Might Ask Myself:

1. If I make a habit of confronting people with their ignorance, why am I surprised that eventually no one wants to listen to me?

2. Can I recall a single moment in my life when I had the courage to risk losing everything by standing up for what is just and decent? What happened?

3. Why do I have difficulty allowing someone *not* to use the help I offer?

# 11

# *Who's Going to Believe Me?*

ONCE MORE JESUS SPOKE to them in parables. "The kingdom of heaven may be compared to a king who gave a wedding banquet for his son. He sent his slaves to call those who had been invited to the wedding banquet, but they would not come. Again he sent other slaves, saying, 'Tell those who have been invited: Look, I have prepared my dinner, my oxen and calves have been slaughtered, and everything is ready; come to the wedding banquet.' But they made light of it and went away, one to his farm, another to his business, while the rest seized his slaves, mistreated them, and killed them. The king was enraged. He sent his troops, destroyed those murderers, and burned their city. Then he said to his slaves: 'The wedding is ready, but those invited were not worthy. Go therefore into the main streets, and invite everyone you find to the wedding banquet.' Those slaves went out into the streets and gathered all whom they found, both good and bad; so the wedding hall was filled with guests.

"But when the king came in to see the guests, he noticed a man there who was not wearing a wedding robe, and he said to him, 'Friend, how did you get in here without a wedding robe?' And he was speechless. Then the king said to the attendants, 'Bind him hand and foot, and throw him into the outer darkness, where there will be weeping and gnashing of teeth.' For many are called, but few are chosen" (Mt 22:1-14).

As she made her way through the near-empty street, Angela was preoccupied with the exciting and dramatic news of the day. A lavish wedding celebration was being held at one of the finest sheep ranches in the area. Everyone in town had talked about the event for days. Every detail from guest list to food was avidly discussed, exaggerated, and used for the game of "best-informed," played with humor (and occasionally seriousness!) by the community folk.

"It could not have happened at a better time," Angela thought. The town needed a captivating distraction from what was a depressing time for everyone: many out of work, governmental harrassment, high taxes, and a crippled economy. Money was scarce and basic necessities were hard to come by. And while there was widespread debate about the injustice of an extravagant party in the midst of such widespread poverty, everyone agreed that the event added spice to otherwise boring and negative conversation.

The street narrowed and curved to the left, passing just outside the community center where laughter and music filled the air. Angela had deliberately taken this detour in order to catch a glimpse of the party. Several others must have had the same idea, for each front window was visited by two or three onlookers peering inside and sharing their views with one another. She listened for a few moments, then decided that because of the growing darkness, she would walk on toward home.

As she glanced ahead, she saw slumped against a side wall and partially hidden from sight a man she recognized as Tobias, a herdsman who worked on several of the area ranches. She hurriedly approached him, knelt beside him, and saw to her astonishment that his hands and feet had been bound together in a rather unflattering way.

"Tobias," she exclaimed, "what has happened to you!?"

He looked dreadfully embarrassed. "I was practicing some new knots and sorta got tied up in the whole mess."

Angela smiled, then frowned.

"You're always joking, Tob. What happened?"

"I'd be delighted to tell you, but," Tobias raised his bound arms, "could you perhaps...?"

"Oh, I'm sorry, Tob. Here, let me get these off." Angela and Tobias struggled to untie first his hands, then his feet. He pulled himself up into a sitting position and leaned against the wall, breathed deeply and looked bewilderedly toward Angela.

"You're not gonna believe what happened."

"Got in a fight and lost?" quipped Angela.

"Hardly!" sneered Tobias. "I guess you've heard about the wedding?"

"Who hasn't?"

"But have you heard about the guests?"

Angela shook her head.

"Well, for reasons not yet known to us ordinaries of the world, there was a boycott of the wedding by many of the other ranchers."

"Boycott?" asked Angela.

"Yes, like a conspiracy to not attend," continued Tobias. "Seems like the father of the bride is not highly regarded round about. So people who were invited just didn't show up."

"I can't believe it!" said Angela.

"Well, believe this, Ange. The old man was so enraged he was determined to fill the hall anyway. So he sends out his sons and drovers to round up everyone in the vicinity—anyone!—and haul them into the wedding. I'm standing across the street talking to some friends when suddenly two giants grab me and escort me into the wedding feast. I've attended a lot of weddings, but this was the first time I went as an arrested guest!"

Angela was laughing. "But at least you got a free meal out of the deal."

"Are you kidding!? You haven't heard the worst of it yet. Once inside, we're handed fresh shirts and coats designed for the occasion and ordered to clean up and dress. I take one look at the man in charge and say, 'Just hold it right there for a minute! I didn't ask to be invited here. Now you're ordering me to dress up if I want to stay where I'm not even sure I want to be in the first place!'"

Angela was feigning disapproval, shaking her finger at Tobias. He continued.

"Right in the middle of my speech, the old man steps in. By now he's so mad he could kill a bear. I could tell I was in trouble. So he orders his thugs to tie me up and throw me out—like a pig! I'm fighting, they're screaming, ropes are flying. Somebody hits me on the head. The next thing I know, you're calling my name."

Tears streamed down Angela's face as she laughed out of control. Tobias was caught in the humor of the scene and joined her in laughter. She paused just enough to stammer:

"Tob, it could only happen to you!"

More laughter.

The two stood and began to walk slowly down the street. Each time they looked at one another they would burst into laughter again.

"So, Tob, how will the story go when we hear about it tomorrow?"

"Mark my word, Angie, by tomorrow they are gonna make it sound like it was my fault and that I got what I deserved! No one will believe my side of the story!"

"Does it really matter, Tob? Aren't people gonna believe what they want to believe anyway? Whenever this story is told, you will still come out on the bottom."

"But what about me? My reputation? My image in the community? Don't I have a right to my dignity?"

"Tob, the people who respect you will ask. You don't have to prove anything to them. The people who don't respect you won't ask and you'd be wasting your time explaining to them. The really hard part is just keeping your mouth shut when you hear about it tomorrow."

"*That,* Ms. Angela, is almost impossible!"

They laughed down the street.

## Questions I Might Ask Myself

1. What are some of the times in my life when I have failed because I did not adequately prepare myself?

2. When I am excluded, why do I blame those who left me out? How might I increase the odds of my being included next time?

3. When things go badly, can I step back and see the humor in the event, thus helping me let go of it?

# 12

# *Get a Job*

AS JESUS PASSED ALONG the Sea of Galilee, he saw
Simon and his brother Andrew casting a net into
the sea—for they were fishermen. And Jesus said
to them, "Follow me and I will make you fish for
people." And immediately they left their nets and
followed him. As he went a little farther, he saw
James son of Zebedee and his brother John, who
were in their boat mending the nets. Immediately
he called them; and they left their father Zebedee
in the boat with the hired men, and followed him
(Mk 1:16-20).

Few summers had gone as well: consistently calm
weather, regular catches of fish, few mishaps with
equipment. In fact, Zebedee could not remember a
time when he felt more hopeful about sufficient
income for his family. He loved his work at sea.
And each year brought him closer to the time when
he could confidently turn the boats, nets, and
bookkeeping over to his two sons, James and John.

He watched them with almost unspeakable love
and pride as they unloaded the last of the day's
bounty. They had not been the easiest of boys to
raise: constantly competing, occasionally fighting,

running off to this festival and that prophet,
skipping their scripture studies for the sake of a
traveling show or preacher. Zebedee and Martha
had on countless occasions been confronted by
neighbors, friends, and family alike about the
provocative antics of their two sons. Yet, both
parents secretly admired the boys and prayed that
their energy and curiosity would eventually
mature into responsible family work and family
living.

As the buyers gradually evaporated with the
setting sun, Zebedee, John and James found
themselves mending a few holes in their nets—
readying themselves for the next day's run on the
Sea of Galilee. Their discussion of the coming
Sabbath was interrupted by the sight of a crowd
gathering on a wharf nearby. In the middle of the
crowd stood a man the three had seen before. He
was a rather refreshing commentator on the Law,
on sacred scripture, and on political issues.

"It's the Nazarene," said James. "Looks like he's
stirring things up again. Those poor lawyers and
priests don't have sense enough to stop trying to
trap him with their clever questions. He makes
fish scales out of them. Not too bright, I'd say."

"Come now, James," challenged his father,
"perhaps our holy men are brighter than you give
them credit. Perhaps they are simply trying to
expose the Nazarene for what he is, a clever radical
who will eventually get ensnared in his own net of
dissension and empty promises. I've seen many
like him before. They make a splash, then no one
ever hears of them again."

"Why, Father?" asked John. "Why do really good teachers and preachers not stay, especially when they are so admired, so sought after?"

"Simple economics, lad," said Zebedee. "They eventually have to get a real job."

The three of them laughed heartily. But even as their laughter was subsiding, Zebedee did not fail to notice his boys eyeing one another—a familiar old tactic of their acknowledging a hidden agenda. A long silence ensued. Zebedee felt ill-at-ease, the kind of feeling that alerts him to a coming storm even though the sky appears clear. He had to ask.

"Okay, you two. What are you not telling your old dad now?"

Predictably, neither James nor John would look up from their netting to their father's piercing stare. The humor was gone, and a serious cloud hung over the men. And though neither son wanted to speak first, John could never hold out from his father as long as James could.

"The Nazarene is different, Father." Even John himself could hear the shallowness of his own words, and quickly added strength to the statement. "I mean, *really* different, Father."

"They are *all* different, John," Zebedee firmly stated.

James waded in to help his brother.

"Dad, we knew you would say that. But we've heard many self-styled prophets ourselves. Even you have commented to mother how clear Jesus is, how protective of scripture he is, how healing he is to people in pain. You yourself suspect a uniqueness in this man."

John quickly added, "And we want to travel with him. He's invited us to follow."

Zebedee's mind was racing. He knew that his sons would never confront him with a request or plan without first thoroughly preparing their arguments. It annoyed him; and it prompted his deep respect for them as well. He looked away and followed the slow landing of a gull on the pier. His eyes began to swim in pools of tears. He could barely speak.

"It's been a good summer. I suppose I can hire some men. Fishing isn't everything."

The silence that followed dug a deep ravine between Zebedee and his two sons. They all felt it. James spoke.

"He's said that we can fish for people."

Anger rushed in and filled Zebedee's throat.

"I'm sure he did!" He felt a bit ashamed. He did not want to end things this way. He continued.

"What about supporting yourselves? We have been blessed with work here. My boats are your boats and my labor was to be your future. Are you sure you want to walk away from what is solidly here, to a life of...of..." Zebedee stopped himself just short of discrediting his sons' plan or the Nazarene they were determined to follow.

John needed to reassure his father.

"We love you, Dad. We appreciate all you have worked for and what you stand for. It's *because* of your example that we are doing this now. You have taught us by who you are to learn, to be skeptical of public opinion, to trust our own judgment, to risk, and above all, to never be held hostage by the past—even though it be good. James and I are not revolutionaries. We have no wild dreams to change the world. What we do have is the dream to make

our faith come alive, to have our faith be relevant
to this brief existence we have—even as fishermen."

"We just want to find out," added James, "what
has gone wrong with life, and what we can do
about it."

Zebedee looked intensely at his two sons, who
were now looking to him for his blessing. He had
argued for their careers. They had argued for their
lives. His sadness at their decision was balanced by
the love and confidence he had in their judgment.
John was right, he had taught them well.

He held open his arms. They embraced one
another.

## Questions I Might Ask Myself

1. When have I trusted my intuition to make a
dramatic change in my life, especially when
things were going well?

2. What were my parents' dreams for me, and have
I felt free to go beyond them?

3. When have I been unwilling to trust a life
decision of my child or close friend—especially
one that seemed so impulsive?

# 13

# *Two Rocks*

WHEN THEY HAD BROUGHT them, they had them
stand before the council. The high priest questioned
them, saying, "We gave you strict orders not to
teach in this name, yet here you have filled
Jerusalem with your teaching and you are
determined to bring this man's blood on us." But
Peter and the apostles answered: "We must obey
God rather than any human authority! The God of
our ancestors raised up Jesus, whom you had killed
by hanging him on a tree. God exalted him at his
right hand as Leader and Savior that he might give
repentance to Israel and forgiveness of sins. And
we are witnesses to these things, and so is the Holy
Spirit whom God has given to those who obey him."

When they heard this, they were enraged and
wanted to kill them. But a Pharisee in the council
named Gamaliel, a teacher of the law, respected by
all the people, stood up and ordered the men to be
put outside for a short time. Then he said to them,
"Fellow Israelites, consider carefully what you
propose to do to these men. For some time ago
Theudas rose up, claiming to be somebody, and a
number of men, about four hundred, joined him;
but he was killed, and all who followed him were
dispersed and disappeared. After him Judas the
Galilean rose up at the time of the census and got
people to follow him; he also perished, and all who
followed him were scattered. So in the present case,
I tell you, keep away from these men and let them

alone; because if this plan or this undertaking is of
human origin, it will fail; but if it is of God, you will
not be able to overthrow—in that case you may
even be found fighting against God!"

They were convinced by him, and when they had
called in the apostles, they had them flogged. Then
they ordered them not to speak in the name of
Jesus, and let them go. As they left the council,
they rejoiced that they were considered worthy to
suffer dishonor for the sake of the name. And every
day in the temple and at home they did not cease to
teach and proclaim Jesus as the Messiah (Acts
5:27-42).


GAMALIEL: Come in, come in, Simon. Here, seat
yourself while I have some food and drink
brought in.

SIMON PETER: Thank you, Gamaliel. I'll just ease
into this soft pile of pillows here if you don't
mind. I'm still a bit sore from the beating we got
in the Council chamber today. I do appreciate,
however, your having spoken so well in our
defense.

GAMALIEL: I wasn't exactly defending you, Simon.
I'm just a little weary of seeing men killed in the
name of 'cleansing the Temple of radicals.' As a
member of the Pharisees, I can assure you that I
fully expect to see your sect die out anyway.

SIMON PETER: Then, thank you, sir, for letting us
die out, rather than be killed off. But why did
you invite me to your home? Some of the
disciples see this meeting as just another trap—a
chance to humiliate me, and divide us. And even

though I know you better than that, I must admit I'm puzzled.

GAMALIEL: Thank you for the trust. By the way, should I address you as Simon or as Peter? I hear both names used.

SIMON PETER: (*Chuckling*) Whatever. Simon is my given name. Jesus gave me the other, "Peter," meaning, as you know, "rock." It started out as a bit of kidding among us. Mark and Judas said I had rocks in my head. I'm not nearly so bright as most of my fellow disciples. Then they kidded me about sleeping like a rock; then, my stubbornness...

GAMALIEL: Let me guess. Stubborn like a rock.

SIMON PETER: Of course. It sorta stuck. It was a pun. Jesus loved puns, using words in a playful, jarring way. Half the time I had to ask what he meant in his jokes, his teasing, his twisting and colorful stories. I loved his stories, and I held onto his words like a fish holds onto a line. I knew this man had me. I knew, even before the others, that he was the Son of God, different from the prophets of old, and that he held a message of life far beyond our comprehension. And when he formally named me Peter, his rock, I and my smiling friends knew the word had a more profound meaning than our humor could fathom. From that day forward, I was Simon Peter.

GAMALIEL: Your story, Simon, reminds me of something I observed about you today at council. You hardly flinched when your band was being

beaten and thrown out. You said nothing. Not a
clue on your face as to anger or bitterness. Might
I ask what you were thinking? Didn't you feel
anything?

SIMON PETER: Oh, make no mistake, Gamaliel.
Those whipping sticks hurt! And we never get
used to it. But by now we've come to expect it.
We've been run out of towns, had dogs put on us,
felt the rain of rocks, curses, threats. Actually, I
was thinking, "Here we go again, Lord. Were you
ever right!" I felt the blows, but I was thinking
about him.

GAMALIEL: I am amazed.

SIMON PETER: Amazed? At what, sir?

GAMALIEL: At you. At your fellow disciples. At *him,*
and his incredible presence in this city two years
after his death. I heard him preach. He was an
absolute genius. I saw crowds of a thousand
people spellbound—including leaders of the
Temple, Roman intellectuals, lawyers. I
witnessed his execution. I knew he was buried
and I've heard rumors of his reappearance. Much
of that I can set aside as wishful thinking and
clever story-telling. But what I cannot dismiss is
*his* stubbornness. He won't go away! Jesus is like
a rock in the sandal of every member of the
Sanhedrin, every Pharisee, every priest, even
our Roman landlords. We kick out the rock. The
next day it's there again. Why? How? What is the
tenacity of this dead teacher that keeps you
going—you and your hard-headed group of Jesus
followers?

SIMON PETER: (*Laughing*) Gamaliel, I wish I knew.
I don't. I really don't know. The man is as
present to me—to us— today as he was the night
before he was crucified. It is a fire burning inside
of me. Like when I was a boy and my father, my
brother Andrew, and I accidentally discovered a
deep hole in the lake. Huge fish! Bigger than we
had seen before. We quickly altered our nets and
learned how to hold them. My father told us to
tell no one. But I burned inside with an
excitement I could not contain. I had to share the
wonderful discovery with others in our village, or
I would burst!

GAMALIEL: Did your father beat you just short of
your life?

SIMON PETER: Actually not. He later confessed to
me that he knew how impulsive I was and that I
would never be able to keep such a secret. My
father was smarter than I thought. And now, it's
the same fire inside me. I've discovered a deep
hole, not in the lake, but in the very fabric of our
Law, in the sea of life itself. It holds truths
bigger than we ever imagined. And I don't even
know what net to use to contain them.

GAMALIEL: What truths, Simon Peter? What truths
are bigger than the Law and our Tradition? For I
have sensed that there must be more to our lives
than obeying the mind-boggling array of laws
and precepts and customs that so touch every
aspect of our days and years and that we are in
some way held hostage by those very same
rituals. We are good; we are obedient; we are
loyal. And we are stagnant to the point of near

death. Our emptiness has become a rage against a world we no longer feel a part of, and we direct that rage toward anyone foolish enough or bold enough to expose the shallowness of our faith.

SIMON PETER: I suppose I should feel honored to be ranked among your more irritating targets?

GAMALIEL: You are, Simon. So tell me, what truth so burns inside you that you would daily risk arrest, torture, and death?

SIMON PETER: I wish Andrew or John or Matthew were here. They speak and write so much better than I. For me, Jesus is the truth that burns inside of me. He is the bridge between God and mankind, not through fear and obedience to law, but through love. His is a love that captures the spirit of law and life, open to the unexpected. He was unashamed to say he was the very Son of God, blessed by God to demonstrate the power of faith, and willing to risk rejection and death as the small price to pay for being passionately alive.

It is like being on the sea when no one else dares being there, casting your nets for the sheer joy of it, and returning home with a sense of having risked all without the slightest promise of a single catch. That, my friend, is fishing! That is the spirit burning inside!

GAMALIEL: I doubt, Simon, that you need your brothers to speak for you. I have no trouble hearing either your message or your enthusiasm—which seem to be the same.

SIMON PETER: That's it! That's it, Gamaliel! They are the same! And that is what is so difficult to define or express. It is not a place like the Temple; it is not a set of laws, or doctrine; it is not me, nor is it all of us together as a group. It is a spirit—the Spirit—of life, of aliveness, of excitement. It is Jesus. The Son of God, filled with the Spirit. Jesus taught us by his words and life what it is to be in union with God and with humankind as a single act of love for life.

GAMALIEL: I wish I had known him better. Just listening to you stirs something in me, a longing, a curiosity. Yet, I am a product of my own history and I must be who I am. In a way, I envy you, Simon. To have lived with this Nazarene must have made it so much easier for you to catch fire, so to speak, to his enthusiastic message.

SIMON PETER: (*Laughing*) On the contrary, Gamaliel. I don't believe I've ever been more troubled, confused, or scared in my life!! Certainly I was hooked from the beginning. But I fought—inside—everything Jesus did and said. I questioned his sanity. I doubted his timing. I couldn't for the life of me understand his meaning of a kingdom not of this world. I am a very literal man, Gamaliel, and I cannot tell you how many times my fellow disciples fell laughing at my questions, my conclusions, my struggling misunderstanding of Jesus. I was terrified of dying like him. I denied I was his follower. Later, I thought that "twelve" had to be preserved, so we elected Matthias. Only recently has it become clear to me that being Jewish is not a requirement for living the life of the Christ. No, Gamaliel, it has not been at all easier for me.

GAMALIEL: Then there is a struggle awaiting anyone who is drawn toward the teachings of your community of believers.

SIMON PETER: Yes. And it is a struggle that never ends. Jesus is a teacher of contradictions. He challenges us to challenge ourselves over and over again. And just when you think you've finally understood something, it is already outdated for you. The Spirit within is a renewing Spirit. Every reality of love is in a constant state of imminent loss. There is no final peace.

GAMALIEL: Then, tell me, Simon, if I were to learn more of this Jesus, what starting place would you recommend to me? What story or symbol would you offer to me that captures the heart of his message?

SIMON PETER: A wedding.

GAMALIEL: A wedding?

SIMON PETER: Yes, a wedding. He loved weddings. He spoke of them often. A wedding is that coming together of two in a committed love, open to the unknown future, and dedicated to carve out of faith a life together that is different from and grander than either could know. It is an act of courageous uncertainty. Start with a wedding. And when you do, imagine two columns of stone rising up then arching toward one another and wonder what makes the arch possible.

GAMALIEL: The center rock, of course. The keystone.

SIMON PETER: And that stone, Gamaliel, the keystone, is my favorite symbol of Jesus.

GAMALIEL: (*Laughing*) Simon, you could *only* have been called Peter by him.

SIMON PETER: (*Laughing*) I know.

## Questions I Might Ask Myself

1. Where is my fire of excitement that burns in order to give me direction in my life?

2. When I hide from or snuff out my excitement, do I do it out of fear of losing control, out of fear of being ridiculed, or out of fear of being child-like again?

3. Where is my courage? When have I been willing to persevere for what I believe in, surrounded as I may be by people who disapprove or threaten me?

# 14

# *Impulse*

IN THE MORNING, WHEN he returned to the city, he was hungry. And seeing a fig tree by the side of the road, he went to it and found nothing at all on it but leaves. Then he said to it, "May no fruit ever come from you again!" And the fig tree withered at once (Mt 21:18-19).

P art of the beauty of living in a semi-desert region is that of scarcity. Water is highly regarded, never wasted. Food is simple, prepared daily, incapable of being stored for more than a few days. And clothing must be suitable for extreme temperature changes from the day's heat to the night's biting chill.

Fuel is another of the desert's sought-after riches: to cook meals, warm bodies, heat water for cleaning or bathing, and finally, light the darkness. These basic necessities depend on the labor of the little people of every desert community. And, as is true in every society, these little people, lowest on the community's social chart, are the very ones who glue the entire structure together, promote its success, then are ignored and dismissed as an embarrassment to the bigger, more important members of the human pyramid.

Like Claudia. At fifty-one, with skin as dry and wrinkled as old leather and hair still as black as charcoal, she was striding like a woman half her age along a dusty road toward Bethany, just outside of Jerusalem. Across her shoulder was an equally old sack containing a thin cloak, bread, and strands of rope. She walked with a cypress staff, not waist high like many travellers, but one that stood as tall as she. She called it her multi-use friend, balancer, defender, load-carrier. She said that her staff generated respect from local thugs who might otherwise take advantage of her diminutive size and only apparent weakness.

Through her years of gathering and selling firewood—first with her husband, now alone— Claudia had become a veritable expert on wood. She admired the beauty of pine groves in the lower hill ranges, the fragrance of juniper, and the stubbornness of cedar. She had lived among the mountainous fir, and she had watched craftsmen work the lines and colors of cypress into furniture and fishing boats. That was her favorite— cypress—tall, hard, and precious, like her staff.

From a professional point of view, she had little use for other trees in the region. Palms were good for dates, but yielded no limbs for gathering. Fruit trees, protected and nurtured all year long, briefly yielded their bounty, then became local decoration again. Of no use to her were those domesticated varieties, because their owners jealously guarded not only the trees' fruit, but their dead limbs as well.

For Claudia, a stand of trees was either a
business resource or someone else's pet. She
needed wood to collect, bundle, then sell in local
communities. And today she was headed for a
grove of pines just outside of Bethany, along a road
that left the trees largely hidden from travellers.

Reaching the summit of a hill, she glanced down
at a gathering of travellers near a turn in the road.
It was a welcome sight, for she had talked with no
one the entire day and her trade depended on
meeting and making regular customers. As she
approached the group, she recognized a familiar
face or two and could hear that a debate was in full
swing. She listened respectfully as she lowered her
sack and sat on a rock outside the circle, all the
while being distracted by a rather small, dead tree
nearby. Possibly the day's income, she thought. But
something else about the tree made her uneasy.
She decided to listen, rather than wonder. Aaron, a
large, burly man, was speaking.

"I tell you, it was as alive yesterday as I am
today. Seen it with my own eyes. And my boy seen
it too! And look at it now. Dead like it had been
that way for a month."

Another cut in. "It was the preacher—him and
his band of admirers. It's all over Bethany. Word
has it he made a big fuss at the Temple in
Jerusalem, beat up on some people, cursed them.
Then he came by this fig tree here, still mad, and
cursed it too! Man's crazy. Possessed, if you ask
me."

"That's it!" thought Claudia. "It was a fig tree."
She had passed it dozens of times in her wandering
trade. She recalled how she did not particularly
like the taste of figs, how scraggly were the tree's

limbs, offering no shade, and how poorly its wood burned. Not much use for fig trees.

"But why?" asked another in the group. "Why would he destroy a perfectly good tree? I heard he was a man of peace, of love, of respect for life. It makes no sense."

Claudia, now feeling she had sufficiently established her membership, spoke up.

"Maybe he was just having a bad day...." She deliberately let the statement lie there like a desert spider, ready to be stepped on.

Several heads turned her way and one spoke. "Claudia! Where did you come from? Welcome. And what are you suggesting?"

Claudia shyly shrugged her shoulders and poked her staff into the gravel between her sandals.

"Like I said. I saw him several times, heard him preach, watched him cure folks." Then she raised her head to the collective eyes. "But he's got one heck of a temper! Only last week when I was at Temple I was putting my last two coins in the offering plate, looked up, and I heard him just blister some of the Pharisees for their pompous ways."

Several in the group chuckled. She continued.

"Got no tolerance for pretenders, no patience for show-offs, not a word of kindness for our idiot priests who can't see the forest for the trees."

The landowner's wife stepped forward. "But it gives him no right to kill my fig tree!"

"Oh, come on now, Owna," interrupted another, "you never liked that tree in the first place. It was too close to the road, you never fertilized it, and even though it looked Okay, its fruit was sour—when it ever had any."

Aaron spoke again. "But it's still crazy. No sense to it. We've all been around him and it doesn't fit what he preaches. There must be something here we're missing—some lesson, some message, some truth that is not immediately obvious to us. There's got to be a logical explanation for this!"

"Why?" asked Claudia. "Why do you insist on looking for something that's not there, Aaron? You men are all alike. Either everything fits nicely together and you consider yourself clever for understanding it, or it makes no sense and you get angry about it, dismissing the issue as beneath your mental dignity. My, my, aren't we arrogant?"

The crowd laughed—everyone except Aaron, who was a bit embarrassed. He defended his ego:

"I suppose, then, that you, Claudia, stick-stacker and prophetess of wisdom, know better?"

"Not better, kind sir, but different," she responded. "If I've learned anything in my brief existence, it is that not everything is explainable, not all events are good, and no person is the same from one day to the next. The preacher is a man of passion. He feels deeply and he behaves in surprising ways—sometimes violently. Can't we grant him what he grants us: to be perfectly human in all our strengths and weaknesses? Can't we allow him what he allows us: that we go to extremes at times, that we destroy what we love, and that we occasionally do impulsive things that we later regret?"

"But why *my* fig tree?" asked Owna.

"Why not?" countered Claudia. "You, too, are looking for what's not there. Look at it this way. It might have been an oak tree, or a camel, or an entire town. Elohim thought nothing of wiping out whole cities when He got mad! This man picked a fig tree. Makes no sense, but it could have been worse."

Everyone laughed.

"So I should consider myself fortunate?" said Owna. "I suppose then that you'll want my dead tree—to cut and sell?"

"No, thank you," responded Claudia. "That dead fig tree makes better fuel for thought than it does for fire. Besides, you and I need to let stand at least two symbols of the world's impulsiveness and nonsense."

"Two?" asked Owna, puzzled.

"Yes," said Claudia. "This tree—and men."

The hills echoed the group's laughter.

## Questions I Might Ask Myself

1. Why am I so unwilling to recognize how much hurt and damage I do when I react impulsively around people I normally care about?

2. What is it that sets me off, makes me out of control? What is that recurring event in my life?

3. What part of me is so vulnerable to that event, the part of me that I should protect *others* from?

# 15

# *No Escape*

THEN I SAW A great white throne and the one who sat on it; the earth and the heaven fled from his presence, and no place was found for them (Rev 20:11-12).

The assembly calls Mr. Judas Iscariot!"

He did not know who had spoken, but Judas responded to the authoritative voice by rising from his bench and standing at attention. He couldn't remember having sat on the bench in the first place, or where he actually was. He knew his name, Judas Iscariot. But where he was, or why, or how he got there were all blanks in his racing mind.

The area was brightly lit. Whether he was indoors or outside was not immediately discernible either. Around him stood and sat what seemed like hundreds of people—all different in color and costume. He felt a chill of nervousness sweep over his entire body as he scanned the crowd for a familiar face. He found none.

The unseen speaker announced, "Please approach the chair, Mr. Iscariot."

Only then did Judas notice a slightly elevated chair some fifty meters in front of him surrounded by more people talking in small groups. He began to walk slowly in the direction of the chair. As he grew closer he felt his nervousness changing into fear, until he was close enough to make out the appearance of the man sitting there. Terror now was enveloping his whole being. For there, sitting before him, was a man who looked exactly like himself. Judas glanced from side to side, then turned completely around. His confusion was reaching a peak of overwhelming pain when the man spoke.

"Hello, Judas. Your confusion will dissipate as we get on with these proceedings."

Horrified, Judas was hearing the sound of his own voice coming from the seated man! He decided to risk a question. "Are...are...are you G-God?"

Around him the crowd, now focused on his presence, chuckled under their breaths.

The man smiled and folded his hands in his lap. "No, not hardly, my friend. I am Judas Iscariot, son of Simon Iscariot."

Judas closed his eyes and opened them. He shook his head violently. He touched his face with both hands, looked down at his feet, then looked directly forward. "But *I* am Judas Iscariot, son of Simon. Then you...you must be me?"

Still smiling, the seated Judas responded. "No, not exactly, Judas. You are the final summation of the rich life you had lived. I, on the other hand, am but a part of you. I am your Judgment. And I am here to perform your—and my—last duty."

"Last du-duty?" Judas asked fearfully. The fog inside of his head began to lift. He felt a tightening in his throat, saw a rope above him. He remembered running, screaming, faces, the Sanhedrin hall, silver coins, the Paschal meal, the eleven others, Jesus. "Am...am I dead?"

"No, Judas," his Judgment responded. "True, you died—a technicality. But as you can see, you are very much alive. You are more alive now than you have ever been."

Judas understood. He felt the first moment of solidness come over him since he had gotten up from the bench a few moments ago. Nevertheless, he could not shake the profound bewilderment of having a conversation with his own image and likeness. Perhaps he was having a dream, perhaps a vision. He considered that he had finally gone mad and was caught in the nightmare of his own desperate and self-destructive life. He could not be sure, yet.

He reached for more clarity. "Then, sir, Judas"— he couldn't believe he was giving in so quickly to the image in the chair—"then is this the final judgment he spoke about?"

"I cannot know," responded Judgment, "if this is *the* final judgment, but it certainly is your judgment. It is a general accounting of your life as you lived it within the limits of your understanding, your skills, and the opportunities given you."

"Does this mean," asked Judas, "that this general accounting, as you call it, will determine my fate forever? Will I be rewarded or punished as a result of this hearing? Is my goodness or badness as a human hanging in the balance for all eternity?" He wished he had not used the word "hanging."

Judgment got up from his chair, stepped down to the level of Judas, turned, and began to pace back and forth, his hands held behind his back. Judas took note that he used to pace this very way when pondering a serious question. Judgment stopped in front of Judas and smiled.

"No, not exactly, Judas."

Judas felt some annoyance at the response and risked a challenge.

"Just a minute, Sir Judas, or whoever you are! If you are Judgment, my Judgment, why do you keep saying 'no, not exactly'? Don't you know? Isn't judgment about having the solution, the right answer, the conclusion of a question?"

Judgment smiled, then answered. "No, not exactly. Sorry, I had to say it. Actually, I, Judgment, am highly imperfect and nowhere near a final solution or answer. I am about the practice of living in a real world that does not allow for perfect solutions or right answers. I am about the business of trial and error, experimentation, learning, and eventually wisdom. We, you and I, are here to discuss things much more important than your goodness or badness. But more about that later. Now, let's get on with it. Are you represented by counsel?"

"I am here," responded a voice from Judas' left side.

Judas turned and was startled to see another image of himself.

"Who...who are you?" he asked, almost afraid to hear the answer.

"I am Judas Iscariot, son of Simon Iscariot, your Counsel and your Defense. I will help you respond to Judgment, and I will present explanations on your behalf."

Defense stepped closer to Judas and placed a hand on his shoulder. Another wave of confusion passed through Judas, but for the first time he felt some degree of protection and safety with this new mirror of himself.

"Then...then," stammered Judas, "you are me also, and you will speak for me if things go badly?"

Defense responded. "I will answer to..."

Another voice broke in from a distance. "To whatever charges are brought against you, Judas, by me, your Accuser!"

Again Judas flinched at the familiar sound of his own voice, this time coming from a man looking like himself, standing to the right of Judgment's chair.

Accuser continued. "I, Judas Iscariot, his Accuser, am ready, Sir Judgment."

"Then, proceed," ordered Judgment.

"Wait, wait, wait!" shouted Judas. "What's going on here? You can't do this! You're trying to confuse me and accuse me, and then pass some judgment that may hurt me forever! I won't let..."

Accuser broke in as though he still had the floor. "The first charge is that of blaming others for the predicaments you create—as you are doing right now, Judas. The second charge is that of theft. Third, misuse and misappropriation of community property for your own self-aggrandizement. Fourth, disloyalty. Fifth, cowardice. Sixth, self-destruction. And seventh, littering a public place with your own bowels—this last being of such a minor issue, that I beg your Judgment to dismiss it summarily."

"So be it," responded Judgment.

Judas stood stunned and speechless. The charges had become reminders of significant events in his life. The scenes were filing through his mind, and he was helpless except to review them. He wanted to say something—anything—to answer the charges.

"With all due respect to the charges being levied against us," said Defense, jolting Judas from his stupor, "I'd like to say a few things on our behalf."

"Please proceed," invited Judgment.

"Thank you. I, we, Judas was not a bad man. In fact, during his life he was zealous in his dreams for liberation of his people from oppression. He aligned himself with and worked diligently in the cause of freedom and spiritual awakening led by the Nazarene. He boldly tried to warn their leader of his potential political undoing and sought to have him chastised and rebuked as an unsuccessful revolutionary.

"I wish to have entered into the record of Judas Iscariot's life that much of his indiscretion, irresponsibility, and selfish behavior can be attributed to a difficult childhood, being raised in poverty, being fed the hopes and dreams of a messiah and growing up under the punitive control of abusive, foreign powers. He wanted only three simple things in life: a comfortable living, overthrow of the government, and establishment of a kingdom he could help rule.

"Even amongst the Twelve he held a position of financial responsibility, directed the procurement of necessities and managed the distribution of resources. He was the only Judean in a group of Galileans—a minority position that gradually took its toll on him by denying him ever becoming one of the in-group of disciples. In fact, there is not a single recorded word of recognition or appreciation for the three years of service he gave to this band of preachers in his position of business manager. It was a thankless job. And not a single note of regret or sadness was mentioned after his departure from the group."

Judas was impressed! Never before had he heard his life outlined, explained, and defended in such a positive manner. He folded his arms and held his head high as he glanced toward Accuser, almost expecting him to collapse in apology. Instead, Accuser remained silent, but Judgment spoke up.

"Thank you, Defense. You have eloquently stated in the most positive light the broad outline of Judas' life. Yet several issues remain which I would like to state in question form.

"First, a man's early-life experiences certainly influence and even bias his adult behavior and decisions. But are you not attempting to argue that those influences somehow determine his future and therefore remove some responsibility from him?

"Second, does a person's disenchantment with his dream give him the right to destroy that dream for others?

"Third, when someone assumes the responsibility of holding in trust that which belongs to a community, then uses those resources as if he himself owned them, is this just a matter of theft? Or is something more profound at stake here? Aren't we talking more about idolatry— whereby one person holds himself forth as superior to the community, owner of it, and exempt from the rules of trust that hold the community together in mutual respect? Doesn't he become then, by self-appointment, a god?

"And finally, what do we say of someone who takes his own life rather than face the consequences of his misguided zeal and his misinformed reasoning? Does it matter what prompted such a final act? Does the community he leaves behind have a say in the judgment of his self-destruction?"

By now, Judas' posture had wilted from an erect stance to that of a huddled slouch. He trembled as he spoke to Defense.

"It...it doesn't seem to be going well for me."

Defense put his arm around Judas' shoulder and offered some assurance. "Hold on, ol' man. Judgment is just doing his job—and doing it well, I might add. You are feeling accused. We...I...just need to respond to your Accuser."

Turning toward Accuser, he continued. "Are you, my good man, accusing Judas of Judgment's speculations and questions? Are you..."

Accuser picked up the question and responded. "I am accusing you, Judas Iscariot, of the recurring behavior of ascribing to yourself the disrespectful manipulation of other people's lives, of using without permission the resources of others, and of bartering the lives of people as if they were your slaves. I accuse you, Judas Iscariot, of being a fraud as a human!"

Defense raised his hand to speak. "On behalf of my..."

"No!" shouted Judas as he pulled away from Defense. "No. I cannot bear to hear from you, Defense, no matter how well you state my case, no matter what the explanation. I...I know that what

my Accuser has just said is exactly true. I lived
much of my adult life fraudulently. I pretended
friendship, I played the roles, I let no one inside. I
dreamed of power in order to escape my own
emptiness, and I stole, out of my own hunger for
some sense of comfort and peace. I found none.

"On that day when I sold my friend for the going
price of a slave, I knew I could never go back. And
when I realized that I had been duped and used by
others for their own political advantage, I knew I
had no future. My own deceit had been used
against me. I was caught by my own treachery and
I saw the fraud that I was.

"No past, no future. I was in fact a dead man. My
hanging myself was the most authentic and honest
thing I ever did as a human."

A long silence ensued. Judas stood with his head
bowed and his hands clenched. Defense
respectfully waited at his left, while Accuser
remained stern in his expression. Judgment was on
his feet again, pacing. He stopped, took his seat,
and began tapping the chair's arm. He spoke.

"And is this the ultimate fraud, Judas?"

"What do you mean?" asked Judas, looking up.

"Like I said," responded Judgment, "is this the
final con—saying what we all would like to hear?
Are you attempting one last time to save your own
skin because you believe this hearing might
determine your infinite future?"

"I don't know anymore," answered Judas. "I
really don't know."

"And do you think," continued Judgment, "that
the honesty you attributed to your death makes it
any more acceptable to the people who knew you

and loved you? Isn't there a responsibility to your community that remains unaddressed?"

"Yes!" charged Accuser. "There are issues that go beyond self-honesty. You have failed to ever acknowledge that your life is not lived in isolation and that your life is never entirely your own."

Defense responded. "We do not question your charge, Accuser. But you are accusing this man of something he never knew. As we have all established so well, Judas never got beyond his own personal preoccupation. He never even saw the faces of his fellow men, and if it had ever crossed his mind that he *had* any connection of respect or love with anyone, he would not have known how to respond!"

After a brief pause, Judas asked, "Earlier, Judgment, you said that there was something more important here than determining whether or not I was a good man or a bad man. What is that?"

Judgment responded. "What is more important than good or bad are the issues of a willingness to be open, to have eyes to see and ears to hear and a heart to feel the humanity you were born to have, and were invited to learn, in your life. It is the business of closing yourself to life that results in death. You have testified to that today."

"And what is your opinion of me now?" asked Judas courageously.

Judgment smiled again. "My judgment is that you are at this moment open. But the question of authenticity remains open as well. We shall see if you can sustain this position in the midst of the community who knew you and whose lives you touched."

Suddenly Judas felt fear return, gripping him like a cold vice.

"You, you mean they are here? I have to face *them* as well?"

Judgment nodded. Now the crowd of strangers that had been standing around began to take on faces of familiarity. Judas was frozen in fear. For gathering around him were his family, his friends, acquaintances, the Eleven, and yes, Jesus.

As if in one voice, they said, "Hello, Judas."

## Questions I Might Ask Myself

1. Am I my worst judge? If so, why am I so hard on myself about past issues in my life?

2. Why is it so difficult to forgive those who have hurt us and benefitted from our suffering?

3. Does an excellent explanation of our poor behavior relieve us of any responsibility for having done it?

4. How would my life change if I fully appreciated how many people are affected by my behavior?

# 16

# *Supporting Role*

AFTER HE HAD SAID this, he went on ahead, going
up to Jerusalem.

When he had come near Bethphage and
Bethany, at the place called the Mount of Olives, he
sent two of the disciples, saying, "Go into the
village ahead of you, and as you enter it you will
find tied there a colt that has never been ridden.
Untie it and bring it here. If anyone asks you, 'Why
are you untying it?' just say this, 'The Lord needs
it.'" So those who were sent departed and found it
as he had told them. As they were untying the colt,
its owners asked them, "Why are you untying the
colt?" They said, "The Lord needs it." Then they
brought it to Jesus; and after throwing their cloaks
on the colt, they set Jesus on it. As he rode along,
people kept spreading their cloaks on the road. As
he was now approaching the path down from the
Mount of Olives, the whole multitude of the
disciples began to praise God joyfully with a loud
voice for all the deeds of power that they had seen,
saying:
"Blessed is the king
    who comes in the name of the Lord!
Peace in heaven,
    and glory in the highest heaven!"
    (Lk 19:28-38).

Yes, I am a donkey. A member of the horse family, thank you. Usually gray in color, about ten hands at my shoulder—halfway between a large dog and a camel. Great ears, sure-footed, keen eyesight, and for my size, the strongest of my family. I have an incredibly efficient digestive system, meaning that I get a lot of mileage out of a little bundle of hay.

Now, take a look at that camel over there. He's three times my height, got a face that would stop a clock (if clocks existed), smells like a garbage dump, and has an attitude that would compete with any three-year-old human. You've never seen such stubbornness! Granted, he too has a high m.p.b. (miles-per-bundle) rating. But who can afford him? Costs a leg and a hind quarter to keep him fed and housed. Not to mention the racket he creates day in and day out.

Don't get me wrong. I don't want to disdain my fellow creatures. Each of us has a place and a purpose in this brief life of ours. None of us is really better or worse; we're basically just...just... different, you might say.

What annoys me, though, what really hacks me, is that some of us—donkeys, for example—never get the kind of recognition or appreciation we are due. Sounds as though I'm pouting, doesn't it? Okay, so I pout. Camels complain, donkeys pout. But my point is valid, nevertheless. Big is considered better, so I lose out. Loud is thought more important and demanding of attention; camels win again. More expensive is thought to be more efficient, more comfortable, and more reliable. Wrong, wrong, wrong! But who's paying attention to facts?!

That's my point. We donkeys have been around
Palestine, Egypt, and Mesopotamia for over three
thousand years. We have been the steady, reliable,
durable haulers-of-choice across distances and
terrain not fit for an animal. We've made this
country what it is today. We, the companion and
workhorse of the little man, have made it all
possible.

Yet who gets painted on the Egyptian walls?
Who gets carved in stone statues? Who gets written
up in the local tabloids? Who gets counted as a
symbol of a man's wealth? Donkeys? Not on your
life! Camels! Glory mongers if I ever knew any!
Small wonder they are so snooty. Bunch of
egotistical road hogs. Think they're entitled to
preferential treatment. Yuck!

There! I've finally gotten it off my chest. Been
carrying around that load of resentment for many a
day. Normally I don't even pay much attention to
what is going on around me. I focus on what my job
is, where I'm headed, and what the road conditions
are under my hooves. In fact it's my single-
mindedness, my docile disposition, and my stamina
that have made me the cherished companion of the
world's laborers and travelers. I get the job
done—quietly, efficiently, and without fanfare.

Which is why my family and I are rarely
mentioned. We are so much a part of the expected
scenery that we just don't stand out. Sort of like
the supporting cast in everyone else's story.

Take, for example, my great, great, great uncle,
His Donkey. He was there when Abraham was
being tested by God to sacrifice Isaac. It was His
Donkey that got them to the land of Moriah.
Wonderful story, good supporting role. It was

Elohim's blessing on Jacob that resulted in his family wealth increasing—a wealth that numbered many of my ancestors, listed casually as "...and donkeys."

Remember when Job was questioning the wisdom of God? What a story! There they were, back and forth in their argument. And where were we donkeys? Right in the middle of God's own tongue-lashing of Job, pointing out the presence of my great great grandparents—Wild Donkeys—and wondering out loud why they were wild! Wonderful dialogue!

Yes, my family tree goes back through the prophets of old, armies of nations, even kings. In fact, the latest of our kingly duties occurred just a few years ago, back when my late aunt, Their Donkey, was fortunate enough to carry a poor mother-to-be into Bethlehem. Good job, too, and perfect timing: the child-king was born the very night they arrived. *That's* reliability.

And I might add that there were no camels on the scene until months later when three wise gentlemen—tourists—rode in on three expensive dromadaries—late. All six of them were decorated to the hilt (I'm not sure that hilts had been invented yet). Then they disappeared into the morning sun like silent ships.

As for me, I'm the last in a noble line, tied here on a back street in Jerusalem. It's a lovely day. People are filling the streets, waving palm branches in the air, and singing "Hosanna!" O, Wow! Here comes my master. That blanket means I'll be carrying somebody important through the streets. Maybe a king, but probably poor. You won't remember me, Donkey Colt. But you're probably

never gonna forget the man who rides me. Gotta
go. It's my job, you know.

## Questions I Might Ask Myself

1. What is my unique list of qualities I can feel
   proud of, even if possessing those qualities came
   through no effort of my own?

2. Why do I have trouble allowing someone else to
   star in a scene I helped create and support?

3. What is my special role in the great drama of
   life? Am I crediting myself for what I offer to
   others?

# 17

# *Mothers and Sons*

WHILE HE WAS STILL speaking to the crowds, his
mother and his brothers were standing outside,
wanting to speak to him. Someone told him, "Look,
your mother and your brothers are standing
outside, wanting to speak to you." But to the one
who had told him this, Jesus replied, "Who is my
mother, and who are my brothers?" And pointing to
his disciples, he said, "Here are my mother and my
brothers! For whoever does the will of my Father in
heaven is my brother and sister and mother" (Mt
12:46-50).

Sunset in the Galilean foothills is as beautiful as
any place on the earth. Early evening reddening of
the sky is followed by washes of deep orange,
violet, and returning striping of deep blues and
grays. The entire horizon, bereft of clouds, creates
a dome of fiery display that only begrudgingly
allows stars to begin to sneak through.

Sunset is also the signal for the day's stubborn,
dry heat to show early evidence of submission to
the coming night. People are ending their meals,
penning animals or herding them to protected
areas, or visiting along the streets. And the usual

sounds of day are yielding to the distinctive hushed
tones and more evident cries of infants.

Two companions made their way past the edge of
town and strolled along a path bordering the
Galilean sea. They silently absorbed the sky's
beauty and the refreshing new breeze sweeping
across the water. They had walked this way
together for years, hundreds of times, using the
experience to share the day's events and to deepen
a bond that held them in mutual respect, love, and
wonder.

Stopping at a rocky knoll, he turned to face the
sea, breathed deeply, and smiled into the colorful
water before them.

"You know, Mother, I never tire of this place: the
quiet, the smells, a sense of the infinite that
envelopes one here. The sky and the sea come
together in a single sheet of beauty. Only when
night finally falls can you clearly separate the two
again."

She felt a slight chill on her arms—from the
breeze, she thought—and slipped her hands into
the sleeves across her chest. Her eyes were fixed on
the water, as she grinned.

"Why do I have the feeling you are about to upset
me again?" she asked.

"What do you mean?" he teased.

She looked into his face. "You know very well
what I mean, Son. Your father did the same thing.
Start with some innocent observation, knead into it
a little story or scripture reference, then serve it up
to me like a fresh baked slice of bread I am
supposed to bite into. Only, there was a little rock
buried inside. I would bite, hurt my tooth, and he
would comfort me with, 'Oh, I'm sorry dear, can I

help?' Clever man, your father. Clever son. So, out with it: I'm too old to lose any more teeth. "

He laughed, stepped closer to his mother, and kissed her cheek. He put his arm around her shoulder and felt her trembling.

"You're too wise, Mother, for your own good. I know it's been difficult for you. Nothing has turned out like we thought it would. You never remarried..."

"And you never married!" she interrupted. "You're a good carpenter, like your father. His faith was strong, too. Yours is an obsession. You are driven to stay on the fringe of life. I just don't understand..."

"I don't understand it all myself either, Mother," he responded. "Have I hurt you that much?"

She looked back to the graying sky. "No, it's not hurt that I have felt so often. What's so difficult is that you are so...so embarrassing!"

They both laughed. Each of them was flooded with memories of his provocative style, street arguments, accusations of demonic possession, threats of rejection from Temple, women following him about, stories exaggerated to unbelievable heights.

"Okay. I admit to my zeal and my daring and my impatience. But it's not just *I* who was so embarrassing. What about you?"

"Me?" his mother protested.

"Yes, you. You're the one who taught me compassion. I watched you for years take care of the ill—people we didn't even know. I saw you slip coins to beggars, hoping father wouldn't see you. And then you started including me in your trips to the leper colonies, finding lodging for travelers,

collecting clothes and food for the poor and hungry.
My friends used to call us the charity guild of
Nazareth. Not always easy to take, Mother."

"That's funny," mused his mother.

"What?"

"I thought it was you who was nudging *me* to see
what was happening all around us. Your father
and I taught you to pray, but it has always been
the intensity of your faith and the amazing effects
of your presence and touch that inspired me to be
even more aware of life, and the sacredness of
people in the eyes of Elohim.

"I have watched you since you were a small boy,
caring for insects and animals, breaking up fights
on the street with hardly a word, moving your
teachers to wonderment with your questions. It is
you who helped me see that there was more than
met the eye."

"But it was you," protested her son, "who felt so
responsible for the well-being of others—like the
success of the wedding last year. Not me!"

His mother laughed. "I just asked for your
intervention. I had no idea what would happen." In
a more serious tone, she added, "By the way, did
you?"

"Know what would happen in advance?" asked
her son.

"Yes," she answered.

"No. No, I did not know. Nor have I known in
advance the outcome of so many events in my life. I
have only been able to see that something different
*must* happen in that moment of necessity, or that
moment of loss, or that moment of faith—your
faith, theirs, mine. It's what father used to say
many times when..."

"Wait, wait, wait!" his mother cut in as she held his arm and pensively laid a finger against her nose. "I know what you're referring to. He said, 'Don't just let life happen: make it happen!'"

The two remained silent for quite a while, watching gulls skim the water's surface as stars began to break through the darkening sky.

"Now," said his mother, "what were you leading me into when you started describing nightfall earlier? What are you about to make happen?"

Her son took her hand and looked into her eyes. "Mother, my life is in danger. Like John, many are being killed. And it's not safe for you. They will seek you out, trying to find me."

She smiled as she reviewed her son's serious face—a face looking more like his father's each year. "So why are you warning me about what I already know? This is your mother you're talking to. Mothers know these things. People talk; I listen."

"What are they saying?" he asked.

She playfully poked him in the chest with her finger.

"That you are a trouble-maker, a prophet, a lunatic; and like your cousin, John, you could lose your head. They're saying that your father would turn over in his grave if he knew what you were doing. They say they pity me and wonder what my secret sin is that I am being so punished."

He held his mother close, saying to her softly, "I'm sorry you have to go through all this, Mother. But I can only be who and what I am. I would never have wished this on you."

She pulled away, and held his shoulders tight in her hands, lovingly chiding him.

111

"Listen here, young man. That's what a mother is for—to watch, to love, to be embarrassed, to hurt, and to eventually lose her son."

He smiled at her. "And that's what a son is for."

"What?" she asked.

"To bring his mother grief."

They laughed and held one another.

## Questions I Might Ask Myself

1. What must happen in order for me to grow up enough to be friends with my parents?

2. Am I struggling against my children or my students eventually becoming my friends and teachers?

3. When is the last time our family celebrated those who, before they died, touched our hearts and made us better people?

# 18

# *Holy Day Inn*

IN THOSE DAYS A decree went out from Emporer
Augustus that all the world should be registered.
This was the first registration and was taken while
Quirinius was governor of Syria. All went to their
own towns to be registered. Joseph also went from
the town of Nazareth in Galilee to Judea, to the
city of David called Bethlehem, because he was
descended from the house and family of David. He
went to be registered with Mary, to whom he was
engaged and who was expecting a child. While they
were there, the time came for her to deliver her
child. And she gave birth to her firstborn son and
wrapped him in bands of cloth, and laid him in a
manger, because there was no room for them in the
inn.

In that region there were shepherds living in the
fields, keeping watch over their flock by night.
Then an angel of the Lord stood before them, and
the glory of the Lord shone around them, and they
were terrified. But the angel said to them, "Do not
be afraid; for see—I am bringing you good news of
great joy for all the people; to you is born this day
in the city of David a Savior, who is the Messiah,
the Lord. This will be a sign to you: you will find a
child wrapped in bands of cloth and lying in a
manger." And suddenly there was with the angel a
multitude of the heavenly host, praising God and
saying,

Glory to God in the highest heaven,
and on earth peace among those whom he
favors.

When the angels had left them and gone into
heaven, the shepherds said to one another: "Let us
go now to Bethlehem and see this thing that has
taken place, which the Lord has made known to
us." So they went with haste and found Mary and
Joseph, and the child lying in the manger. When
they saw this, they made known what had been
told them about this child; and all who heard it
were amazed at what the shepherds told them. But
Mary treasured all these words and pondered them
in her heart. The shepherds returned, glorifying
and praising God for all they had heard and seen,
as it had been told them (Lk 2:1-20).

W hat was that?!" shouted Lydia as she sat up
from a dead sleep. Beside her, Tobias grumbled
and turned, his snoring only temporarily
interrupted. Lydia cupped her hand to her ear and
listened intently in the dark. "It *is* a baby, wailing
its little lungs out. Tob, Tob?" She shook her
husband several times.

Without opening his eyes, Tobias snapped, "No
babies checked in tonight. Probably one of the
guests' donkeys."

"That's it!" said Lydia. "The young couple with
the donkey. We were full and offered them the
corner stable that was not used. She was
pregnant—more than we thought. She's having her
baby. I'll be right back."

Tobias grabbed her arm. "Hold on, hold on. She's
all right. When I made my rounds before bed, there
were two other women guests talking to them and

offering help. You need your rest for tomorrow. We've never been so busy."

Lydia yielded to her husband's urging and settled back against her straw pillow. It had been an exhausting day. The whole town of Bethlehem was crowded with people, and every night saw a complete turnover of guests in their lodging place. Her husband, Tobias, was a hard worker, maintaining the rooms in good repair, ordering hay for the stables, keeping a reliable ledger. For Lydia, running a lodging place was her opportunity to meet interesting people and to hear about the world's happenings through the reports of guests. In fact, their lodging place had become a community center for news and meetings—a statement of success in the small town.

Tobias was fast asleep again, as Lydia lay in the dark listening to the quieting cries of the newborn. She decided she would look in on the couple in the morning, and she fought off feelings of shame that a stable was all they could offer the couple that night. She dozed off.

"What was that?!" shouted Lydia, as she sat up in bed for the second time. A loud banging on their apartment door answered her question. She shook the snoring mass next to her:

"Tob, Tob, wake up! Someone's at the door!"

Without responding, Tobias rolled out of bed, threw a blanket around himself, and headed for the door.

"Hold on! Hold on!" he grumbled. He opened the door to an obviously angry face—one of their guests. Before Tobias could speak, the man growled.

"Do something! I've paid for our room; I expect to be able to sleep. *Do* something!"

"About what?" asked Tobias, now fully awake.
"About the singing!"

Lydia joined her husband at the door. "It *is* singing!" she said. Tobias looked at his wife and said commandingly: "I can *hear* the singing, okay?! Did you register a choir today?"

"*You* register the guests! How do *I* know if we have traveling minstrels if you don't tell me?"

"Look, folks," barked the guest outside the door, "you two have your fight some other time. For now, would you quiet down the noise in the field behind the corner stable?"

The three listened momentarily to the distant singing.

"It *is* coming from the field, where the sheep herders camp for the night!" said Lydia.

"The fields?" exclaimed Tobias. "That settles it! We're just proprietors, sir, not the local constable. Nothing I can do about it. Besides, it's probably some traveling messengers bringing some joyful tidings of an important event. Happens around here all the time. We're sort of a news center around here. We'll check with the shepherds later to hear what's going on. I suggest cloth for your ears. Good night, sir."

The disgruntled guest reluctantly departed, leaving Lydia and Tobias listening to the not unpleasant chorus fading in the early morning darkness. They returned to bed, pulled a blanket up to their chins, and exchanged questioning glances.

"I don't know either," said Tobias. They eventually fell asleep.

"What was that?!" shouted Lydia, bolting awake again. Door banging echoed through the room.

Tobias was sound asleep. Lydia got up and raced to the door so that her husband could continue sleeping undisturbed.

"Hold on! Hold on!" she shouted, thinking how she was starting to sound too much like Tobias. She flung open the door and was startled to find a gathering of guests there.

"Is your husband here, madam?" demanded one of the guests. Lydia felt her back straighten.

"He is," said Lydia, "and so am I: What can I do for you?" She felt her jaw tighten. For several seconds a stare-down locked everyone in place. Lydia felt competent to handle questions of guests and was not about to wake her sleeping husband again. The four men facing her were not accustomed to women in charge. The men backed down.

"There are sheep bleating outside every window!" protested one.

"And dogs barking!" exclaimed another, waving his fist.

"And people milling around and chattering nonstop. It's the middle of the night, for heaven's sake!" whined a third.

Lydia cupped her hand to her ear. "It *is* sheep—and dogs—and those shepherds, they never do that. Usually more respectful of our lodge and guests. Something strange is going on. Okay, go back to your rooms, and I will talk to them."

She quickly closed the door before anyone else could speak. Her mind was racing. Perhaps Tobias should be informed. And because he knew the local shepherds better than she, perhaps he would prefer to handle the noisy disturbance. She sat on the bed and began to gently shake him. He gargled in his sleep.

"Tob, Tob. Wake up. There's something strange happening outside, and—"

Suddenly there was more banging on the door. Impulsively, Lydia shouted, "What's that?!"

This time Tobias sat up and yelled, "We've a bunch of lunatics around here! What now?!"

Together they hurried to the door and opened it. There stood a crowd of over a dozen people, arguing with one another in loud and angry voices.

Tobias raised his arms over his head: "Hold it! Hold it! What in the world is happening?"

"That's what *we* want to know!" shouted a complainer. Others joined in the clamor.

"Yes!" protested another. "Babies crying, music in the middle of the night, a sea of sheep waking the dead, sheep dogs yelping. And now this!"

"Now what?" asked Tobias.

"Now, camels! Grunting and snorting!"

Lydia cupped her hand to her ear.

Tobias looked at her and spoke simultaneously with her: "It *is* camels!" They laughed.

"And several nicely dressed Easterners, with footmen," added a guest.

Tobias and Lydia continued to laugh.

"Seemed normal when we ended the day!" laughed Lydia.

"The place is going crazy!" laughed Tobias.

One of the crowd stepped forward. "Look! I don't see what's so funny. We just want to sleep. Is that so much to ask?"

"Not at all, not at all, my good man," chuckled Tobias. "But that's the point, we want to sleep too. And none of us has even bothered to find out what is going on around us. Life is happening, and we'd rather sleep."

"Tell us in the morning!" quipped the spokesman. "For now, we don't *want* to be bothered; so just be responsible enough to keep it all apart from us!"

Lydia smiled at Tobias. "You're right, Tob. Let's go be a part of it: we can always sleep."

The two left their room together.

## Questions I Might Ask Myself

1. Why have I missed magical moments in my life by attending to routine duties rather than paying attention to the people around me?

2. How can I learn how to define a disruption in my daily life as an opportunity rather than as a nuisance?

3. What can I do to better hear and deal with others' disappointments, without feeling responsible or apologetic?

# 19

# *Easy Work*

FINALLY, BE STRONG IN the Lord and in the strength
of his power. Put on the whole armor of God, so
that you may be able to stand against the wiles of
the devil. For our struggle is not against enemies of
blood and flesh, but against the rulers, against the
authorities, against the cosmic powers of this
present darkness, against the spiritual forces of
evil in the heavenly places. Therefore take up the
whole armor of God, so that you may be able to
withstand on that evil day, and having done
everything, to stand firm. Stand therefore, and
fasten the belt of truth around your waist, and put
on the breastplate of righteousness. As shoes for
your feet put on whatever will make you ready to
proclaim the gospel of peace. With all of these, take
the shield of faith, with which you will be able to
quench all the flaming arrows of the evil one. Take
the helmet of salvation, and the sword of the spirit,
which is the word of God (Eph 6:10-17).

It was the same old red and blue carpet; same
boring, maroon curtains hanging behind the bare
platform stage; same dead, imitation ivies on dull
wood lattices at the wings. Straight-back chairs in
parallel rows faced a yellowed pink wall. A hideous

imitation of a chandelier hung at the center of the
enormous meeting room, while in a corner stood a
courtesy table with its predictable warm water and
cold coffee.

A full membership of over 665 was in attendance
today, standing in small groups, smoking,
exchanging horror stories of the past year. A
serious, even somber mood was already evident as
the crowd began to seat themselves and watch
President Seil approach the podium. He stood
motionless, eyes fixed ahead, and waited for the
noise to evaporate.

"Ladies and gentlemen," began Seil, "I want to
welcome you all to this annual meeting; and with
your permission, I would like to dispense with our
usual rituals in order to go immediately to the
urgent business at hand. As you know, we will
have three committee reports, followed by an open
discussion on the question: do we really exist?"

A clamor immediately erupted on the floor.
Several members stood up, shouting. Others waved
their fists. A dozen more filed from a row and
marched in what was obviously a pre-planned
demonstration toward a rear exit, only to find it
locked and guarded by their own colleagues. Seil
banged his gavel several times.

"Gentlemen, Ladies! Please take your seats.
You'll have a chance to be heard."

As the crowd quieted, Nomed, an elderly and
highly regarded member, rose to his feet with his
arms beating the air.

"This whole thing is absurd, Seil! Preposterous!
This meeting is either a tasteless joke or a
deliberate slap in the face of a brotherhood that

has labored together for thousands of years. You make us look backwards!"

Again the room burst with excitement, shouts, applause, jeers, and shoving. The president banged on the podium.

"Ladies! Gentlemen!"

They quieted.

"I am not entirely in disagreement with you, Nomed. But Natas, our leader, has commanded it. And we will proceed. Now! The chair recognizes the first committee report. Senkrad, please come forward. And please keep the reports brief, ladies and gentlemen."

Senkrad rose and approached the podium. He slowly opened his bound ledger and began to study it as though for the first time. Without raising his head, he looked over the top of his horn-rimmed glasses to the waiting group.

"President Seil and honorable colleagues. As chairman of our research committee, I am pleased to report that belief in the demonic and participation in evil has never been stronger in the world."

An applause rippled through the crowd. Senkrad continued,

"Until recently, our work has been documented largely by folktale, art, and an occasional religious sect hellbent on rebelling against local custom and established churches. Now something more concrete and verifiable has been occurring: Jesus and his disciples have identified our presence and they have..."

The entire audience was on its feet screaming. Seil hammered away with his gavel. The tumult was deafening.

"Gentlemen! Ladies!" bellowed Seil as he turned toward Senkrad. "You know the general command, Senkrad, and you have deliberately violated it: you shall not say his name unless forced to address him directly!"

Senkrad was unmoved. He continued. "Hundreds of us have been denied the right of possession; our leader confronted Jes...uh...him, several times and failed to sway him, even at his death. Our best contact, Judas, useful for a moment, rejected our offer in the end. Even Paul is causing us havoc: the mere touch of his garment sends us running.

"In a word, there is a growing body of evidence that not only do we exist, but that our presence is visibly experienced by and written about among the believers and followers of...of him."

Applause.

"Thank you, Senkrad," said Seil. "Now..."

A voice interrupted from the center of the room.

"May I please address the chair, President Seil?"

There stood the austere and ancient figure of Madame H'taed. Seil nodded approvingly.

"My colleagues," continued H'taed, as she faced the group, "with all due respect to research, I wonder if we can entrust proof of our existence to these rather, how shall I say, inconsequential episodes of exorcism? Is this a statement of significance, or power? Personally, I consider it rude and demeaning to simply be identified as the victims of some trick or cure. Pure prattle! Either we *are* evil, or we are nothing! Either our role is more profound, or we stand here today pitifully trying to justify our existence on the word of a handful of dusty preachers!"

The audience grumbled and nodded in agreement.

"Well stated," replied Seil, "and you have, Madame H'taed, anticipated our next committee report. I now call upon Lord Feiht."

Feiht rose from the front row and approached the podium. A respectful applause accompanied him. He surveyed the room, then addressed the gathering.

"Comrades. The task of your policy committee— that of establishing and maintaining our identity— is not an easy one. Several important questions were raised.

"First, are we the same as evil, or does evil exist apart from our existence?

"Second, is 'evil' just another word people need for explaining misfortune?

"Third, is misfortune just another misunderstanding of the natural randomness of the universe, the normal flow of good and bad?

"Fourth, is bad the final appeal of a lazy mind to whatever disrupts someone's routine, comfort, or sense of safety?

"Finally—and we think this issue strikes at the heart of whether or not we exist—is our identity bound up with doing evil, or are we called to a much higher order, a question suggested a few moments ago by Madame H'taed."

"Yes! Yes!" shouted the crowd, as it rose to its feet in applause and cheers.

President Seil shouted above the noise: "And has your committee reached a conclusion?"

"We have," responded Lord Feiht. "Our task is that of *distraction*. If we exist at all, then we exist for the purpose of distracting the world from the message of Jes...uh...him, to us. Our task is that of convincing the world that they must focus on avoiding evil, defeating the devil, exorcising demons, and battling daily the forces of darkness in their lives!"

Cheers and applause erupted from the crowd. Feiht continued.

"Our presence in the world is to encourage a preoccupation with fraud, deceit, dishonesty, power, control and escape from death. Our task is to so galvanize the people of earth into thinking about what they must be battling *against* that they will miss completely his message of what they should be living *for!* Their guilt, their fear, their search for the enemy both within and without will so distract them that he will fail from lack of an audience!"

The hall exploded with cheers, screams, and laughter.

Seil watched with approval as his colleagues celebrated the committee report. Feiht returned to his chair, and Seil banged his gavel again.

"Gentlemen! Ladies! Gentlemen!" The gathering slowly calmed. "Thank you. We have one final report: that of the social action committee. Madame Etah."

A stout, round-faced figure rose from the audience and walked quickly to the podium. A gleeful smile greeted her colleagues as she raised her hand for silence. She began.

"Honorable Seil, followers of Natas, my co-workers. The question put before our committee was one of *implementation*: how are we best to accomplish the goals outlined so beautifully by Lord Feiht? What is the most effective way to achieve total preoccupation with evil and total ignoring of his message of love? Our collective answer is this.

"First, we shall work toward the continued infantilization of the human race, encouraging their over-indulgence, their win-lose thinking, their emotional immaturity, their abdication of responsibility, and their recourse to blame.

"Second, we shall reward their successes in wealth, power, and dominion over one another—confirming their secret belief that there exists the deserving and the undeserving.

"And finally, we shall concentrate our efforts not in petty struggles of individuals and families, but in the national and international institutions that they believe in. The arenas of politics, religion, health, government, education, law, and business will be our finest fields of endeavor. These structures of society have the most insidious and debilitating effect on the spirit of humans, and it is all done under the disguise of rules, order, criteria for membership, profit, and purity. We don't have to create instruments of evil: they already exist! There is our home, those very institutions which by definition exist to fight us. They are our finest allies!"

The entire audience was on its feet again, applauding, screaming, waving their arms.

"Brilliant!" "Superb!" "Unbeatable!" they screeched.

Above the clamor, Etah bellowed:

"The church, naively thinking it is the same as his believing community, and exercising its dominion over, and collaborating with, these other institutions, shall reign as our most protective

host, while parading itself as our most ardent
enemy. If the church exists, then *we* exist!"

The members went crazy with celebration. Walls
vibrated from the noise. The hideous chandelier
rattled. Chairs were overturned from wild dancing
and shoving and self-congratulations. President
Seil watched with obvious approval, waving to
members, nodding to Etah, Feiht, H'taed, Nomed,
and Senkrad. The conference had been a success.

No one was noticing.

No one was noticing a gray figure standing near
the old wooden lattices at the wings. Arms crossed,
piercing eyes, rigid in posture, he watched the
jubilant members. He turned, and as he began to
make his way to the stage center, applause of
recognition rippled through the room. President
Seil announced:

"I give you our leader, Lord Natas!"

Everyone stood at attention and continued their
applause. Natas approached the podium; silence
enveloped the room. He began:

"You have done well today, my brothers and
sisters. I commend your reports. Yes, the
instruments of tyranny and despair lie in the
hands of organized people themselves. They make
our work easier. And so long as the church exists,
we exist.

"But this I warn you: the day the church stops
believing in itself and starts believing in him, the
day the church stops taking itself so seriously and
takes people more seriously—that day, when the
church is transformed into his people, then we
shall cease to exist."

"How will that ever happen?!" shouted Nomed.

Natas smiled. "It will happen only when they finally realize that the dignity of a single person is more sacred than all the churches and religions of the world—an event not likely to ever occur!"

The celebration continued—and continues.

## Questions I Might Ask Myself

1. What have I done to struggle with my own thinking about evil? To what degree have I merely accepted other opinions or pronouncements on the existence of evil in the world?

2. How do I daily compromise my values, my ethics, my responsibility to my fellow human beings, thus promoting by my laziness the presence of evil in the world?

3. To what degree am I prepared to hold myself accountable for the inhumanity promoted by the business, agency, organization, group, institution or church in which I claim membership?

# 20

# *It's Not Fair*

FOR THE KINGDOM OF heaven is like a landowner
who went out early in the morning to hire laborers
for his vineyard. After agreeing with the laborers
for the usual daily wage, he sent them into his
vineyard. When he went out about nine o'clock, he
saw others standing idle in the marketplace; and
he said to them, "You also go into the vineyard, and
I will pay you whatever is right." So they went.
When he went out again about noon and about
three o'clock, he did the same. And about five
o'clock he went out and found others standing
around; and he said to them, "Why are you
standing here idle all day?" They said to him,
"Because no one has hired us." He said to them,
"You also go into the vineyard." When evening
came, the owner of the vineyard said to his
manager, "Call the laborers and give them their
pay, beginning with the last and then going to the
first." When those hired about five o'clock came,
each of them received the usual daily wage. Now
when the first came, they thought they would
receive more; but each of them also received the
usual daily wage. And when they received it, they
grumbled against the landowner... (Mt 20:1-11).

Anyone can plant a garden, follow the advice of friends on care and feeding, protect the young plants from adverse weather, and enjoy the noticeable flavor of homegrown vegetables. In almost every part of the world, home gardening is an achievable and predictable undertaking.

But suppose a gardener—having met with a summer success that attracts the envy of neighbors and adds to their tables—suppose that same gardener purchased a hundred acres of land, bought seed and equipment, and tried to duplicate his success the following season. He has, in effect, left the realm of gardening and entered the realm of farming. The rules have changed. The weather is now totally uncontrollable. Timing for planting and harvesting is more critical, with the window of success more narrow. And what was once an individual endeavor has now become a cooperative venture of farmer and hired laborers.

Like generations before and after him, Justin had dreamed of having his own farm some day. But because of few resources and a series of poor growing seasons, he was currently limited to hiring out as a field hand to other farmers. He loved the work, he didn't mind moving from one part of the country to another, and he was free to do so because he had no family to look after.

The sun was high as Justin approached a lone tree beside the road he was walking. Shade was a precious commodity in these parts, and a mid-day rest seemed well deserved. He dropped his sack of meager possessions next to the tree, wiped the sweat from his face, and glanced in all directions. Fields of ripened wheat surrounded him. Work was possibly at hand.

Just as he was about to lie down next to the tree, a wagon appeared far down the road. As it approached, Justin considered asking for a ride, as it was going in his direction. Still some distance away, the driver started waving to catch his attention. Justin reached for his bag as the wagon stopped beside him. The driver shouted.

"Looking for work, sir?"

"Maybe," responded Justin, as he set the stage for friendly negotiation.

"Five a day starting immediately, and everyday till the crop's in."

"Paid daily?" asked Justin.

"Every night," assured the driver.

Justin heaved his bag onto the wagon: "I'm in!"

He climbed on as the wagon jolted forward, and the two rode in silence to the harvest area further down the road.

Justin needed no instructions as to the task at hand. Joining some twenty other laborers he cut wheat, stacked, tied, collected, and loaded for the rest of the day. The work was invigorating as well as tiring. At dark, when the foreman called for a halt in the work, the men gathered up their belongings and headed for a small tent set up at the edge of the field. Justin noticed, but then dismissed as unimportant, the fact that more workers were present at the farm owner's tent than when he had joined the crew.

"Come in closer," began the owner. "I wish to thank you all for working so hard to harvest my crop. We need to get it in as soon as possible. As a courtesy, I would like to have the men who started with me early today come forward first and receive their agreed-upon wage of five coins."

The group of men shuffled about as twelve laborers made their way to the front and began collecting their wages. The sound of clinking coins was interrupted by the third man in line.

"Master, I object to what is happening," he began. The owner looked up in amazement, and before he could speak, the laborer continued.

"Sir, in talking with one another through this day, we know that you have hired men who have not worked a full day, yet you are paying them the same wage as we who have labored through the entire daylight hours. It's not fair."

Tension filled the air. Not a sound could be heard in the tent. The farm owner stood up and glared at the worker. Everyone waited.

"My good man," the owner began, "you agreed to the wage of five, which I am willing to pay you. There is no injustice here. Why should I now change my part of the bargain just because, just because…"

He was searching for a conclusion of his thoughts. The men were restless. Justin had been in similar moments before: unclear agreements, wage disputes, and worst of all, fights. He feared one might break out now and cause him to lose his pay. He spoke up from the group.

"Just because you now have new knowledge and a different perspective."

The men turned to Justin in stunned disbelief—a laborer defending the owner!

"Explain yourself!" encouraged the master.

Justin hesitated, knowing he was now in the middle of a fight anyway. He continued to his fellow laborers.

"You, sir, made a decision based on what you considered a fair agreement, a decision to work the full day. That contract holds true regardless of the master's need to hire more men throughout the day. His urgency has nothing to do with your agreement."

The men began to discuss among themselves the points of the debate. Moments passed before the owner spoke:

"I suppose that my generosity has created some feelings of unfairness among you. But I have neither lied nor deceived any of you. My offer remains. Thank you, sir, for helping to clarify the matter."

Each man in the first group collected his wage. Then the owner announced.

"Now, will the men who arrived at mid-day come forward and collect their five coins." Ten men, including Justin, began moving toward the front. At once, Justin was struck with the now obvious fact that several additional men, as yet unpaid, had been hired late in the day—and at the same wage of five coins! Suddenly he felt confusion and anger welling up inside of him. He now found himself in the more-work-for-same-pay group. He felt embarrassingly rebellious.

"Just a moment!" Justin shouted toward the pay table. "I thought I was among the last laborers hired. But there are men here who barely worked a single hour today, and you will be paying them the same as us! I withdraw my support of you, sir. You truly are unfair!"

Some men joined in the shouting. Others laughed out in a ridiculing fashion. The foreman called for silence. The owner spoke.

"Which is it that I am, young man," he asked, referring to Justin: "fair, or unfair? Does it depend on the matter at hand, or does it depend on whether my generosity is to your advantage or not?"

Laughter erupted among the workers. Even Justin could not squelch a grin in the face of such humorous exposure. His attitude had in fact been altered by the sudden change in position he found himself, rather than the owner's position.

"And I now ask all you good workers," continued the master, "am I not free to keep my word with each of you—each of you who at some time during the day was delighted to receive such good wages?! I cannot wait until the season is over before deciding when is the perfect time to till and when to plant. None of us is granted the luxury of having large chunks of time in which to examine the amount and circumstances and future outcomes of events in our lives.

"I have farmed all my life. And this I know to be true: that while I use the wisdom of the past, I must stand behind the decisions I make this day. I cannot afford to wait until I am fully prepared, fully informed, totally fair or absolutely certain before I take action on what I must do today. My integrity stands on how responsibly and honestly I act toward you today. That, my friends, is how I am able to sleep guiltless each night!"

The group of laborers nodded to one another in agreement and approval of the owner's words.

"Sir," Justin inquired above the chatter, "when tomorrow comes and you again hire us to continue the harvest, shall I sleep through the day and arrive for work only in the last hour?"

Laughter erupted among the men. The owner and his staff joined in. Then the owner offered:

"My good man, you may fool me once by taking advantage of my generosity. But not twice. What is it that you want: a chance to work or dismissal to the road?"

"Work!" responded Justin.

The owner smiled. "Then I shall see you in the morning."

## Questions I Might Ask Myself

1. In what ways am I going through my life lazily letting jobs find me, then complaining that I'm always treated with disrespect and unfairness?

2. When have I ever defined for myself what work I prefer to do, developed the necessary skills, then gone out and made my career happen?

3. What can I do to remain confident that the decisions I made in the past were made with the best information available to me then, and that hindsight does not diminish in any way the validity of those decisions?

# 21

# *In the Service of God*

NOW THE FESTIVAL OF Unleavened Bread, which is
called the Passover, was near. The chief priests and
the scribes were looking for a way to put Jesus to
death, for they were afraid of the people (Lk 22:1-2).

Caiaphas walked briskly through the double
cedar doors of the palace assembly, accompanied by
his father-in-law, Annas. As reigning high priest of
the Sanhedrin governing council, Caiaphas was
both religious leader and chief legal administrator.
Since religion and law were indistinguishable from
one another, and since nothing in the kingdom
went untouched by both, Caiaphas was King
Herod's most powerful man in the nation's capital,
Jerusalem. Only in issues that concerned capital
punishment did he have to answer to the civil
governor of their land that was currently controlled
by the Roman Empire, that governor being Pontius
Pilate.

Two major political parties made up the
Sanhedrin: Pharisees and Sadducees. Solid in
theology, experts in the Law, and dedicated to the
preservation and execution of sacred scripture, the

Pharisees were respected for their learning, their religious observance, and their wide range of interpretation of the Law. The Sadducees represented the aristocrats of the kingdom, were more practical in their theology, and were interested primarily in social order and international relations. Both groups were surrounded by their administrative assistants, the scribes.

Even though the assembly had been hastily convened, more than fifty of the seventy members were in attendance due to their presence in the capital for Passover. Everyone knew the purpose of the meeting, and several near-polite debates were in process as Caiaphas took his chair before a gold-draped wall. He studied several small scrolls handed him by his scribe, then glanced up to the men standing around. They grew silent at his cue.

"May the blessing of Almighty God be with this council," he intoned in solemn chant.

"May he guide us in truth and justice," they replied.

"Gentlemen," began Caiaphas immediately, "there is no one here who is uninformed of the Nazarene and his cult. For three years we have watched his movements and heard his preaching throughout Judea and Galilee. Only yesterday reliable sources reported he brought a family member back to life after four days dead. And we know he will probably make a grandstand presentation during the celebrations this week. We have no time to lose."

The assembly erupted in loud argument and shouting. The high priest raised his hand for silence.

Gamaliel, a ranking Pharisee, spoke.

"Your holiness, and my brothers, I would urge that this assembly proceed with extreme caution and deliberation. This is no ordinary self-styled preacher or trouble-maker. He is well-grounded in the Law; he has the respect of many people, and he is politically brilliant."

Many of the members nodded and grumbled in agreement.

"I think it would be wise," said Caiaphas, "if we started with what might be some formal charges brought against the Nazarene thus far. Scribe, please read from the scroll."

His scribe began. "Thus far, he is charged with: First, preaching in synagogues without proper certification from this Council.

"Second, healing the blind, crippled and diseased without a license.

"Third, distributing food without a permit.

"Fourth, working on the Sabbath while—"

"Rubbish!" interrupted a Pharisee, Joseph of Arimathea. "The countryside is crawling with preachers and healers. We have neither the time nor the energy to make those charges stick."

Caiaphas arose, snatched the scroll, and held it above his head.

"Then try this on for size, you dimwits. He's getting high ratings in the polls by calling himself not a preacher or prophet, but the very Son of Elohim! Are any of *you* sons of God? He's pushing the idea that he's the Messiah; are there any claimants in this room? Simply stated, gentlemen, the carpenter is making us look like fools!"

A hush filled the room. Then Saul, a Sadducee, spoke.

"If he were the true Messiah, he would be a duly-appointed member of this council. He would be with us, rather than embarrassing us."

"Oh, please, Saul!" retorted Gamaliel. "If he were a part of this Council, he could not possibly be a Son of God! A Messiah would not stomach the mediocrity, cowardice, or amoral air that we share with one another. We can't even agree among us what we stand for or who the enemy is. So we take aim at whoever speaks the loudest, like John, or the most brilliantly, like Jesus. It's not this preacher that puts us to shame. It's ourselves!"

Among the jeering that followed, a single laughter sliced through.

"Our brother here," said old Annas, "would perhaps have us invite the Nazarene in for a political consultation? You seem to forget, Gamaliel, that despite our shortcomings, we are the law of the land, and he is threatening both the law and the land. Politics is the business of government. It works best when the people overlook our flaws and believe we have the power to maintain stability in their lives. This preacher magnifies our flaws and is slowly stealing our power to control. He is too dangerous to let live."

"So now we have broached the subject," said Caiaphas, taking charge again. "Our common folk don't really understand the issues at stake. Offer them a little tax deduction, give them some free medical care, or throw them a free meal now and then and they will follow anyone! But the Nazarene goes further. He is inviting them to question our whole tradition and our political stability."

"Wonderful!" sneered Nicodemus, another Pharisee. "Isn't that the same conclusion this Godly Council came to concerning the last twenty-seven men we found irritating? Let's just have one more murdered in the name of law and order!"

Screaming and shoving and rageful threats erupted in the assembly. Four of the Pharisees and two scribes stormed out of the room in protest. Caiaphas and Annas conferred together as the tumult continued for several minutes. Solomon, an elderly Sadducee, walked to the center of the hall and stood with his hand raised for silence. Slowly the noise abated.

"My brothers," began Solomon, "I am an old man and I have seen seventy-six years of unrest, poverty, and subjugation of our nation. It is our law and our tradition that holds us together as a people. This preacher speaks of a kingdom that he shall rule, and even though he insists it is spiritual in nature, can we really expect the masses of devout but uneducated people to understand that distinction? Can we afford to risk misrepresentation of him by the news mongers of this land? Can we allow the Romans to think there is even a hint of a threat to their control? Can we allow this self-styled Galilean political renegade to curse us in public, to foretell the destruction of the Temple, and to claim Sonship with the same God *we* are commissioned to represent? This kind of division will bring the Roman sword down upon our necks!"

Most of the assembled cheered with approval the words of Solomon. A few stood silently with arms folded and heads lowered. Caiaphas stared at this small group of dissenters dispersed throughout the

hall. He had attended school with Gamaliel and
Joseph. He and Nicodemus were boyhood friends.
His love for these brothers was such that he could
not respond to Annas' and Saul's signals to end the
council discussion while they held the upper hand.

"Nicodemus," said Caiaphas, "you obviously have
more to say. Please do so."

Nicodemus slowly walked around the council,
pausing to look into the eyes of a fellow legislator,
then moving on to another, then another. He faced
the group with uplifted hands:

"What are we doing? Who are we? Have we
become so self-serving and arrogant in our
positions of religion and government that we are
more committed to preserving our office than we
are to the God we worship and the people we
serve? Is Rome really the problem? Do we keep
throwing the lion an occasional dog so that he
won't eat all of us?"

"My brothers, I offer to you that the lion is not
Rome. The beast that is slowly eating away at our
nation is our own blindness. The beast is our
refusal to see the shallowness of our faith, the loss
of vision in our lives, and the murderous shortcut
to our moral decay!"

Members shouted curses and insults at
Nicodemus. He continued without pause.

"Your protest proves my point, gentlemen. No, I
am not a devotee of the Nazarene. But who in this
room has not been privately moved by his words?
He says what we cannot say, because we have sold
our souls to safety, security, order, and the
numbing predictability of law."

Caiaphas broke in. "Regardless of how
imperfectly you describe our positions in this

council, brother Nicodemus, we can only be who
and what we are."

"Yes!" exclaimed Gameliel. "And that is the most
tragic part of all. We have all lost our freedom to
think or to see beyond our lots in life. Jesus signed
his own death warrant when he took the step to
become a public challenger to our Law and
tradition. He knew that he would be killed. We are
trapped in having to kill him because *that* has
become our law and tradition. Pilate is trapped in
having to approve it because he can't afford
another embarrassment. Judas is trapped by his
near-sighted attempt to stop his leader from being
executed.

"And here we stand, going through the motions
and reading our lines, trying to convince ourselves
that we are really doing something important,
acting as if we were in charge. And we are not. We
are deaf and blind children, clutching without
question the frayed edge of our mother's old and
tattered garment."

"What then would you have us do, Gamaliel?"
asked Caiaphas with an unusual softness in his
voice. "I, too, have on occasion wondered about
such questions, but I am utterly bewildered as to
whether the choices we can conceive have any basis
in the real world of politics, government or religion.
The Nazarene dares to say out loud what we have
secretly thought. He speaks of a spiritual
revolution. We live more practical lives, which
cannot bear such change."

"Perhaps," offered Joseph, "that is why he
accused us of being dead already!"

"Enough!" shouted Saul. "I will not stand being
cursed for what I and this governing body believe

in and live diligently to preserve! If a man, *any* man, makes himself to be *the* son of God, he has by definition defiled the first law of Moses, regardless of his wisdom or his popularity. And I charge you, my brothers, and you, Caiaphas, to do your duty to have him put to death!"

The room filled with shouting and arguments. Nicodemus raised his hand and received a final nod from Caiaphas to speak.

"Then before this council passes judgment, please remember one thing. Prophets have a tradition of opening our eyes to see beyond our present limitations; we have a tradition of killing them because of it. This is neither the first nor the last time we, the leaders of a nation, have chosen to silence the voice of truth and vision. May Elohim forgive us our self-deceit!"

For several moments the men stood in place, silently reviewing the arguments, privately assessing their duty. Many would recall for the rest of their lives how time seemed to have stood still during that pause. Others would recall the safety they each felt that a group was required for such a decision, while a few, convinced of their divinely-appointed positions, had not a glimmer of doubt.

Caiaphas rose to his feet. "It is expedient that one man should die for the people so that the whole nation might survive intact. Do I hear your voice?"

Enough responded: "He shall die."

"Then it is decided," said Caiaphas. "For thirty pieces of silver, the price of a slave, he shall be arrested, tried and executed."

In solemn chant he led: "In the service of God."

Many responded: "In the service of God."

143

## Questions I Might Ask Myself

1. When were the times I have sacrificed someone else's feelings, position or integrity in order to save my own skin?

2. When have I ever been courageous enough to stop or at least challenge a group decision that was demeaning or hurtful to an individual's welfare?

3. When have I ever had the self-honesty to question political statements and actions, without being caught by the hook of self-interest or benefit?

# 22

# *You Can Have It All—Maybe*

AND THE LORD GOD planted a garden in Eden, in
the east; and there he put the man whom he had
formed. Out of the ground the LORD God made to
grow every tree that is pleasant to the sight and
good for food, the tree of life also in the midst of the
garden, and the tree of the knowledge of good and
evil (Gen 2:8-9).

So the Lord God placed Adam and Eve in the
Garden. In the Garden they had everything they
needed to be content: enjoyable work to tend the
Garden, companionship, sufficient food and shelter,
the challenge of the seasons, the wonders of life,
and the loving protection of the Lord God.

"Everything I have here is yours, except this one
tree," said the Lord God, "the tree of the Knowledge
of Good and Evil. Of this tree's fruit you may not
eat, or you both shall surely die."

Both Adam and Eve wondered at this
prohibition, but it was not a problem for them—at
least not initially. They were content. But as time

went on, they began to discuss how their
peacefulness and joy might be even greater if they
also had access to the special tree.

Eve, being a rather adventuresome woman, was
especially drawn to the central tree. She, like
Adam, longed to know its secret. One day as she
stood viewing the tree, a serpent approached and
urged her to risk finding out.

"Don't be afraid," the serpent said, "for when you
finally *have it all*, you shall be like God, and your
happiness will be complete!"

The opportunity seemed just too good to pass up.
Eve hesitated for a moment, then she took and ate
the fruit of the forbidden tree. And she shared it
excitedly with Adam.

The rest is history. Yes, a change did occur. Now
they *had everything*. There was nothing left to
their imaginations; there was no more adventure,
no self-denial, no struggle, no longing, no dreams.
They *had everything* now, and they each felt a
sense of emptiness at the same time.

The emptiness became sadness. The sadness
made them feel ashamed. Adam and Eve were
profoundly confused. They withdrew and hid in the
Garden.

So when their friend, the Lord God, was walking
in the Garden the next day, he called out:

"Adam! Eve! Where are you? Why are you
avoiding me?"

Adam answered from where they were hiding:
"We did not want you to see us so ashamed and
unhappy, Lord God. We have no explanation for
our sadness. We thought we would be even happier
today."

"My poor Adam. My poor Eve," wept the Lord God. "You have learned only too late that peace and joy are yours only if you do not have everything. To yearn and to dream is what life is all about. To struggle and wonder and never know in advance the next moment is life itself. But when you eat the poisonous fruit of *having it all*, then you truly die inside, and you lose the very gift of life—as has now happened."

"Please don't be angry with us," they pleaded. "We couldn't help ourselves."

"And besides," challenged Eve, "you knew we could not avoid that tree forever! Why did you place it there for us to be tempted by it? It's not all our fault!"

Adam tried to stop her. But even as he did, the Lord God smiled, for God secretly admired her spunk.

"No," the Lord God responded, "I will not blame you. But neither can I allow you to go backwards to the time before you tested my wisdom. You both shall always have my love and my protection. And because I love you, I will once again allow you to yearn and dream. I will *withhold* from you the curse of *having everything*.

"Henceforth, you and your children and all who come after you shall live your lives remembering the Garden which you must now leave. From this moment on, you and they shall always yearn for your beginnings. And you shall eventually die knowing that it can never be yours.

"Each day of your life that you struggle more to clearly define who you are and accept the limits of your knowledge and efforts, then you shall have inner peace. And each day that you demand to be

more, know more, and receive more than you
*are*—on that day you shall again taste the curse of
the forbidden fruit.

"Your emptiness shall remind you of your
demand. Your peace shall remind you of my
promise.

"I shall always love you. I will never desert you."

## Questions I Might Ask Myself

1. How much is enough—in any category of my
life? Am I stuck in the belief that more is always
better?

2. When have I examined the very issues of
"owning," "consuming," "keeping," in my life to
the neglect of "sharing," "giving," and
"enhancing?"

3. What stops me from accepting and celebrating
the present moment of my life, without the
sadness of what once was or the longing for
what might be?

# Epilogue

We, the individuals who live within the events of the bible, wish to thank you for hearing our stories. We hope that you have smiled a little and laughed a little. We hope also that your mind and heart have been provoked into some fresh thinking, not for the sake of changing the world, but for the sake of influencing *your* world.

Remember that your own story, created by you as you move through your brief life, is touched by all whom you meet. Thank you for allowing us to travel a while with you.

# Index of Scripture

# Index of Themes

# *Use* Lord, You Must Be Joking!
## *in Your Faith-Sharing Group*

Now that you've read **Lord, You Must Be Joking!** how can you share it with other members of your community? The companion **Leader's Guide** provides suggestions for moving you and your group beyond the stories and into individual and community faith development. Each lesson plan (one per story) includes discussion questions, personal story sharing, group activities, and prayerful reflection.

Use **Lord, You Must Be Joking!** and its **Leader's Guide** for bible study groups, adult initiation groups, small Christian community groups, retreats and workshops.

## LEADER'S GUIDE TO
## *LORD, YOU MUST BE JOKING!*

*John E. Barone & Eugene J. Webb*

Paper
$7.95
80 pages
$5\frac{1}{2}$" x $8\frac{1}{2}$"
0-89390-310-8

---

*Order from your local bookstore, or use the order form on the last page.*

## Stories for Reflection and Growth

# by Lou Ruoff:

## FOR GIVE
## Stories of Reconciliation

Paper, $8.95, 120 pages, 5½" x 8½"
0-89390-198-9

In this collection of original stories, Lou Ruoff focuses on gospel reconciliation stories: The Prodigal Son, The Unforgiving Servant, Seventy-Times-Seven, and more. Great for homily ideas, for catechesis, or for Re-membering Church sessions.

## NO KIDDING, GOD,
## WHERE ARE YOU?
## Parables of Ordinary Experience

Paper, $7.95, 106 pages, 5½" x 8½"
0-89390-141-5

The author shows you where he finds God: in a bottle of whiteout, in a hand of poker, in a game of hopscotch. These twenty-five stories work effectively as homilies and as ways to find God in everyday life. To help you with your planning, they are accompanied by Scripture references according to the season of the liturgical year.

## PARABLES OF BELONGING
## Discipleship and Commitment
## in Everyday Life

Paper, $8.95, 112 pages, 5½" X 8½"
0-89390-253-5

This collection of stories recognizes the ability of average people to minister to others in their lives just by carrying out their day-to-day activities. Telling these stories will help listeners acknowledge and rejoice in their own hidden giftedness and invigorate your community.

*Order from your local bookstore, or use the order form on the last page.*

## *Stories for Reflection and Growth*

# by James L. Henderschedt

### THE LIGHT IN THE LANTERN
### True Stories
### for Your Faith Journey

Paper, $8.95, 124 pages, 5½" x 8½"
0-89390-209-8

Award-winning author James Henderschedt has a gift for telling imaginative stories. This collection, linked to the lectionary, goes beyond facts to the truth of one's faith journey. Use them for personal reflection, homily preparation, or small-group work.

### THE TOPSY-TURVY KINGDOM
### More Stories
### for Your Faith Journey

Paper, $7.95, 122 pages, 5½" x 8½"
0-89390-177-6

These stories turn the ordinary world upside down and inside out. Use them for preaching—they're keyed to the lectionary—or use them in religious education. Your listeners will see themselves in the characters Henderschedt paints so vividly.

### THE MAGIC STONE
### and Other Stories
### for the Faith Journey

Paper, $7.95, 95 pages, 5½" x 8½"
0-89390-116-4

Put the word of Scripture in context with today's lifestyles and the word becomes reality for you. Share them aloud and the word comes to life for your congregation, prayer group, or adult education class.

*Order from your local bookstore, or use the order form on the last page.*

# *More Stories for Faith-Sharing*

**STORIES TO INVITE FAITH-SHARING:**
**Experiencing the Lord Through the Seasons**
*Mary McEntee McGill*
Paper, $8.95, 128 pages, 5½" x 8½", 0-89390-230-6
Based on real life experiences, these stories will help you recognize God's presence in everyday life.

**WHO KILLED STUTZ BEARCAT?**
**Stories of Finding Faith after Loss**
*Kristen Johnson Ingram*
Paper, $8.95, 96 pages, 5½" x 8½", 0-89390-264-0
Nine stories that confront situations of loss head on and uncover res-urrection experiences in every segment of life.

**BIBLICAL BLUES: Growing Through Setups and Letdowns**
*Andre Papineau*
Paper, $7.95, 226 pages, 5½" x 8½", 0-89390-157-1
This book of biblical stories will take you deep into your own personal recovery and transform you.

**JESUS ON THE MEND: Healing Stories for Ordinary People**
*Andre Papineau*
Paper, $7.95, 150 pages, 5½" x 8½", 0-89390-140-7
Eighteen imaginative stories based on the Gospels illustrate four as-pects of healing brokeness.

**BREAKTHROUGH: Stories of Conversion**
*Andre Papineau*
Paper, $7.95, 139 pages, 5½" x 8½", 0-89390-128-8
These stories remind us that change ultimately is a positive experience.